Most Lawyers Are Liars

The Truth About Self Employment

Written By

Money Guy and Tax Guy

Most Lawyers Are Liars - The Truth About Self-Employment

Now that you have filed for the right company, set your account books up correctly, let's talk about becoming successful at being self-employ.

How to be Successful At Self-Employment

What Is Self-Employment?

A self-employed person does not work for a specific employer who pays them a consistent salary or wage. Self-employed individuals, or independent contractors, earn income by contracting with a trade or business directly.

In most cases, the payer will not withhold taxes, so this becomes the responsibility of the self-employed individual.

Self-employed persons may be involved in a variety of occupations but are highly skilled at a particular kind of work. Writers, tradespeople, freelancers, traders/investors, lawyers, salespeople, and insurance agents all may be self-employed persons.

Key Takeaways

- Those who are self-employed work solely for themselves and contract directly with clients.

- Self-employment may not be subject to tax withholding, so those who are self-employed are responsible for paying their taxes.

- Self-employment can provide a great deal of job flexibility and autonomy; however, it also comes with a greater degree of employment risk and a more-volatile income.

Self-Employed

Self-Employed vs. Business Owner

Although the precise definition of self-employment varies among the U.S. Bureau of Labor Statistics (BLS), the Internal Revenue Service (IRS), and private research firms, those who are self-employed include independent contractors, sole proprietors of businesses, and individuals engaged in partnerships.

A self-employed person refers to any person who earns their living from any independent pursuit of economic activity, as opposed to earning a living working for a company or another individual (an employer). A freelancer or an independent contractor who performs all their work for a single client may still be a self-employed person.

A self-employed person is not often the same thing as being a business owner. The owner of a business, for instance, may hire employees and become the boss—an employee-owner who operates and manages the business.

Alternatively, a business owner has an ownership stake but may not be involved in the day-to-day operations of the company. In contrast, a person who is self-employed both owns the business and is also the primary or sole operator. The taxation rules that apply to those who are self-employed differ from the employee or a business owner.

Independent contractors, sole proprietors of businesses, and individuals joined in a partnership are all self-employed persons.

Types of Self-Employment

Independent contractors are businesses or individuals hired to do specific jobs. They receive payment only for the jobs that they do. Because they are not considered employees, they do not receive benefits or workers' compensation, their clients do not withhold taxes from their payments for work performed, and equal opportunity laws do not apply to them.

Examples of independent contractors include doctors, journalists, freelance workers, lawyers, actors, and accountants who are in business for themselves. It is worth noting that independent contractors are not just limited to specialized fields. An NPR/Marist poll conducted in December 2017 found that one in five jobs in the United States is a contracted worker as opposed to a full-time employee.

Sole proprietors are the only owners of unincorporated businesses, while partnerships involve two or more self-employed people who form a business together. Independent contractors, sole proprietors, and partnerships often hire a small number of employees to help them with their work.

According to a Gallup survey commissioned by Quickbooks and published in 2019, as of 2017 (the most recent figure as of early 2020), self-employed people and their employees accounted for 28% of the workforce in the United States (including people with multiple jobs who are both employees and self-employed). The industries with the highest rates of independently employed people include agriculture, construction, and business and professional services.

However, the report took pains to point out in an executive summary that "it is important to note this research was conducted before the COVID-19 pandemic, which has clearly impacted the way Americans work today." With the increasing prevalence of Americans working from home or losing jobs due to the pandemic, it's very likely that the ranks of the self-employed have swelled even more.

28%

The percent of the workforce that is self-employed as of 2017 (the most recent figure as of late 2020)

Special Considerations

Taxes for the Self-Employed

A self-employed person must file annual taxes and pay estimated quarterly tax. On top of income tax, they are also, typically, required to pay a self-employment tax of 15.3%. Of this tax, 12.4% goes to Social Security on the first $137,700 of earnings as of 2020 ($142, 800 in 2021) and 2.9%

goes to Medicare tax.

The self-employed person will pay the employer and the employee portion of Social Security and Medicare taxes. Those who make less than an annual net profit of $400 are exempt from paying taxes on that income.

The gig economy, a phenomenon that emerged with digitalization, includes everything from Uber drivers to dog walkers to consultants. There are upsides and downsides to being a gig worker. The advantages are, of course, flexibility and control, but the disadvantages are that there is no guarantee of work, the pay is often low, and there are no employee benefits such as sick leave or a healthcare plan. Gig workers must be disciplined when it comes to paying taxes because they do not receive W-2s and must oversee all tax withholding independently.

Self-Employed Person

Who Is a Self-Employed Person?

A self-employed person is an independent contractor or a sole proprietor who reports self-employment income. Self-employed people work for themselves at a variety of trades, professions, and occupations rather than working for an employer. Depending on the jurisdiction, self-employed persons may have special tax-filing requirements.

Key Takeaways

- A self-employed person is someone who earns their living from any independent pursuit of economic activity, rather than working for a company or an individual.

- The business structures that self-employed people may choose include independent contractors, sole proprietorships, partnerships, corporations, S corporations, and limited liability companies (LLCs).

- Self-employed individuals are highly skilled at a particular kind of work.

- The self-employed have traded the comforts of security for the exhilaration of freedom.

How It Works for Self-Employed Persons

A self-employed person in the United States, as defined by the Internal Revenue Service (IRS), is one who:

- Engages in a trade or business as a sole proprietor or an independent contractor

- Is a member of a partnership involved in a trade or business

- Is otherwise in business for themselves (including a part-time endeavor)

In other words, a self-employed person is anyone who earns their living from any independent pursuit of economic activity as opposed to earning a living working for a company or another individual (an employer). A freelancer or an independent contractor who performs all their work for a single client may still be a self-employed person.

Self-employed individuals may be involved in a variety of occupations but are highly skilled at a particular kind of work. Writers, editors, tradespeople, traders/investors, lawyers, actors, salespeople, and insurance agents may all be self-employed.

Anyone who is self-employed but not an independent contractor may choose a variety of business structures. The most common are partnership, sole proprietorship, corporation, S corporation, and limited liability company (LLC).

Benefits of Self-Employment

The prime benefit of self-employment is freedom: to do something that you love, to set your own hours, to decide which work you will and will not do. If you work from home, you can save money on transportation to the office, as well as on the wardrobe that office requires, and get a tax deduction for the business use of your home (more on that below).

If you are building your own business, you have complete control over how to do that, from whom (if anyone) to hire to how and to whom to sell your product. You are not limited by a salary as to how much money you can earn. Your creativity at solving problems will not be stymied by a boss with limited vision. Finally, there is the sense of pride and accomplishment in creating a successful enterprise that is your domain and yours alone.

Disadvantages of Self-Employment

The biggest disadvantage of self-employment is the uncertainty of risk. You may not be limited in what you can earn, but you are also not guaranteed a certain salary. When you have a bad month or two, you must be able to absorb the losses. You must shoulder all business expenses yourself; there is no turning in an expense report for reimbursement. If you pursue your business by yourself, you forfeit the camaraderie and support of coworkers.

There are also financial downsides. You must pay the employer half of Social Security and Medicare taxes in addition to paying your half. You are not eligible for employer-provided healthcare plans and must instead fund your own health insurance. You have no access to employer-sponsored retirement savings plans, such as a 401(k), and you cannot receive the financial match that an employer frequently contributes to such retirement plans.

There are alternative retirement savings plans available to you, such as the solo 401(k), the simplified employee pension individual retirement account (SEP IRA), and the savings incentive match plan for employees (SIMPLE) IRA, but you must fund them all by yourself. Fortunately, the contribution limits for these plans are higher than 401(k) plans. With a SEP IRA, for example, in 2020 the limit is either 25% of compensation or $57,000, while the 2020 limit for a 401(k) is $19,500. Of course, you must make the money to take advantage of the higher limit.

Because taxes are not deducted from their paychecks, self-employed persons must pay estimated taxes in advance to the IRS on a quarterly basis.

How Self-Employed Persons Pay Taxes

A self-employed person has to file annual taxes and pay estimated quarterly tax.4 On top of income tax, they also must generally pay a self-employment tax, which is a Social Security and Medicare tax for the self-employed that was 15.3% as of 2020 (12.4% for Social Security on the first $137,700; 2.9% for Medicare with no ceiling). A self-employed person can deduct the employer-equivalent portion of the tax to lower their adjusted gross income (AGI). For an individual to figure out if they owe self-employment tax, they must determine their net income and loss from their activities on Schedule C. Anyone who has earned at least $400 must pay the tax.

The self-employed may be eligible to deduct expenses for the business use of their home, known as the "home office deduction." Under specific IRS rules, you may be able to deduct such things as the portion of your insurance, rent, repairs, security systems, and utilities and services bills that was used for business purposes.

Self-Employed Persons: Europe

Individuals who work for themselves in the United Kingdom are classified as "sole traders." If a person runs their own business and is responsible for its success and failure, has several customers simultaneously, decides when and how to work, and has a number of other characteristics, then they are self-employed.

In the European Union, self-employed persons are defined as those "who work in their own business, professional practice or farm for the purpose of earning a profit, and who employ no other persons."

Independent Contractor

What Is an Independent Contractor?

An independent contractor is a self-employed person or entity contracted to perform work for—or provide services to—another entity as a nonemployee. As a result, independent contractors must pay their own Social Security and Medicare taxes.

In addition, an entity that uses the services of an independent contractor is not required to provide them with employment benefits, such as health insurance and employer-sponsored retirement accounts that the entity may otherwise provide to its employees. The payer must correctly classify each payee as either an independent contractor or employee. Another term for an independent contractor is "freelancer."

Key Takeaways

- Independent contractors are not employees, nor are they eligible for employee benefits.

- They do not have taxes withheld from their paychecks but instead must pay estimated income taxes in advance through quarterly payments.

- Freelancers can reduce their gross income using allowed business deductions, thus lowering their tax bills.

- Independent contractors must arrange for their own insurance and retirement.

- The category for independent contractors is extremely broad.

Understanding Independent Contractors

Doctors, dentists, veterinarians, lawyers, and many other professionals who provide independent services are classified as independent contractors by the Internal Revenue Service (IRS).

However, the category also includes contractors, subcontractors, writers, software designers, auctioneers, actors, musicians, and many others who provide independent services to the public. Independent contractors have become increasingly prevalent in the rise of what has been dubbed the "gig economy."

Independent contractors must keep track of their earnings and include every payment received from clients. Clients are legally obliged to issue 1099-MISC forms to their contractors if the amount they paid warrants that expense. If an independent contractor earns more than $599 from a single payer, that payer is required to issue the contractor a 1099 form detailing their earnings for the year.

Independent contractors must decide how much freedom they need versus how much risk they are willing to assume.

How to Pay Taxes as an Independent Contractor

In the United States, independent contractors are considered sole proprietors or single-member limited liability companies (LLCs). They must report all their income and expenses on Schedule C of Form 1040 or Schedule E if they have profits or losses from rental properties.12 Further, they must submit self-employment taxes to the IRS, usually every quarter, using Form 1040-ES.

However, as sole proprietors, independent contractors do not necessarily pay taxes on their gross earnings. Applicable business expenses can reduce their overall tax obligation. The difference between gross earnings and business expenses is the net income, which taxes are due.

For the tax year 2021, independent contractors pay 12.4% in Social Security contributions on the first $142,800 of net income) and 2.9% in Medicare taxes on all net income.4 Single filers must pay an additional 0.9% Medicare tax on self-employment income that exceeds $200,000 ($250,000 for married couples filing jointly).

Some independent contractors may also have to pay state sales taxes if they are creating a product and depending on the product, they are producing.

Pros and Cons of Being an Independent Contractor

The pros of being an independent contractor relate to the greater freedom they enjoy. They can set their hours, pursue work they love, and decide what work they will and will not accept. Those who can work from home may save money on transportation and the wardrobe needed to work in an office. They may also get the home office tax deduction that allows them to deduct the business portion of their bills for such things as insurance, rent, repairs, security systems, and utilities and services.

They have complete control over building their business, from hiring and firing to choosing clients. Unlike employees who have a set annual salary, there is no limit on how much money they can earn. Finally, they can enjoy the sense of pride and accomplishment in building a successful business enterprise that belongs to only them.

The cons of being an independent contractor are related to the risk of going bankrupt and the opportunity cost of a regular career. They are not supported by a regular salary when business is terrible, and their income is unpredictable and highly volatile month over and year over year. This income fluctuation undermines them vis-a-vis banks and lenders for mortgages, car loans, and other types of loans. They are responsible for all business costs—no reimbursable expense reports for them—and if working alone, they lack the support and camaraderie of coworkers.

Independent contractors are not eligible for employer-provided healthcare plans, so they must completely fund their healthcare. They must also pay both the employee and the employer parts of Social Security and Medicare taxes. They are not eligible for employer-sponsored 401(k) plans or matching contributions from those who employ them.

Pros

- Independent contractors can set their own hours and choose their own work.

- They are not limited by an annual salary as to how much money they can earn.

- Often, they can save money by working from home.

Cons

- Independent contractors are responsible for all their business expenses.

- They must fund their own healthcare.

- They are not eligible for unemployment insurance or workers' compensation.

Example of an Independent Contractor

One example of an independent contractor would be an interior designer who works for themselves and has a roster of clients who hire them to decorate their homes. The interior designer might even work on a contract for an architecture firm that employs them to work closely with their clients throughout the building process of a new home.

The designer, an independent contractor, would work out how many hours, payment, and ideas with the architects (who they are contracted to work with) on the project but might collaborate closely with the client during the decorating process. At the same time, the interior designer might be working for other clients and working on various homes simultaneously, versus being an in-house designer and only working for clients of the architecture firm.

While they do have access to some alternative retirement plans, such as a SEP IRA, SIMPLE IRA, and solo 401(k), they must fund these all by themselves, and they have no access to unemployment insurance or workers' compensation payments.

The Bottom Line

Working as an independent contractor can be a wonderful way to earn a living for people who desire flexibility, do not mind inconsistent earnings, and who can manage their time while potentially juggling multiple clients.

In addition, independent contractors must be comfortable with filing their taxes quarterly with the IRS and paying for their own insurance, plus retirement savings. For some, the freedom to choose projects, and the flexibility of working for themselves, make the challenges worth it.

How Do You Become an Independent Contractor?

You can become an independent contractor by working for yourself. Many freelancers in a gig-centric economy transition are independent contractors who work on a contractual basis to provide goods or services. Independent contractors may have a registered legal business name, earn any necessary certifications or licenses, and pay their estimated taxes quarterly to the IRS.

What Is the Difference Between an Independent Contractor and Self Employed?

An independent contractor is the same thing as being a self-employed worker. An independent contractor could be a dentist who owns his own business, for example. The difference between being a freelancer, say someone who knits hats and occasionally sells them at holiday fairs would not necessarily be an independent contractor, as they usually provide a good or service on a contractual basis.

How Do You Fill out a W9 as an Independent Contractor?

If you are an independent contractor and hired by a company or person to perform a service, chances are they will ask you to fill out a W-9 form. You must verify information, including name, address, and tax identification number. All the pages of W-9 are available on the IRS website, which also provides step-by-step directions on how to fill it out.

How Do You Fill out a 1099-MISC Form for an Independent Contractor?

Form 1099-MISC is available on the IRS website for anyone who needs it. There are 17 boxes to fill out on the form, plus you must include the payee's name, address, a tax identification number for both the payee and recipient, plus the recipient's name and address. In addition, the IRS provides step-by-step instructions on how to fill it out.

How Do You Pay an Independent Contractor?

You pay an independent contractor just like you would pay any freelancer either by the hour, by the project, or a flat fee. You can pay an independent contractor by check, Venmo, PayPal, or cash.

Freelancer

What Is a Freelancer?

A freelancer is an individual who earns money on a per-job or per-task basis, usually for short-term work. A freelancer is not an employee of a firm and may therefore be at liberty to complete different jobs concurrently by various individuals or firms, unless contractually committed to work exclusively until a particular project is completed.

Key Takeaways

- A freelancer is an independent laborer who earns wages on a per-job or per-task basis, typically for short-term work.

- Benefits of freelancing include having the freedom to work from home, a flexible work schedule, and a better work-life balance.

- An example of a freelancer would be an independent journalist who reports on stories of their own choosing and then sells them to the highest bidder.

Understanding Freelancers

Typically, freelancers are considered independent workers and may do their contract work full time or as a side job to supplement full-time employment, time permitting. Freelancers, as independent contractors, typically require signed contracts for the job to be done and will agree to a predetermined fee based on the time and effort required to complete the task. This fee may be a flat fee or a per-hour, per-day, or per-project fee, or some other similar measure.

A freelancer tends to work in the creative, skilled, or service sector, such as in film, art, design, editing, copywriting, proofreading, media, marketing, music, acting, journalism, video editing and production, illustration, tourism, consulting, website development, computer programming, event planning, photography, language translation, tutoring, catering, and many more.

Freelancers and Taxes

The Internal Revenue Service (IRS) categorizes freelancers as self-employed. A self-employed worker, unlike an employee of a company, does not have their taxes withheld by the company with which they are doing business. Paying income taxes is, therefore, the sole responsibility of the freelancer, and estimated taxes must be paid in advance in quarterly installments. In addition to the income tax, a freelancer is also subject to the self-employment tax mandated by the IRS. The self-employment tax applies to a freelancer who earned $400 or more in any given tax year. The tax has two components: one for Social Security and the other for Medicare.

As the IRS considers freelancers to be business owners, they must pay self-employment tax as both an employer and employee. Social Security tax is assessed at a rate of 6.2% for an employer and 6.2% for the employee. An independent worker such as a freelancer would be taxed 6.2% + 6.2% = 12.4%, as they are both an employer and an employee. The Social Security tax is only applied to the first $137,700 of income earned in 2020 (this so-called taxable maximum will be raised to $142,800 in 2021). The Medicare tax rate, which is 1.45% for both entities, is 2.9% for the self-employed worker.[4] The total self-employment tax rate that a freelancer must pay is therefore 12.4% + 2.9% = 15.3%.

Freelancers may qualify for certain tax deductions that business owners can claim on their business expenses. According to the IRS, these have to be ordinary and necessary expenses (O&NE) for the operation of the business. This means that a freelancer would not be able to claim a deduction on an expense that they would normally make without the business. Some examples of deductions that can be claimed include home office deductions, such as rent and utilities, the costs of traveling to a job, the costs of entertaining a client, the cost of courses or certifications that directly relate to the business profession, and more.[6]

In the U.S. freelancers do not receive W-2 forms for income tax purposes and instead are sent a 1099-MISC tax form, which typically doesn't include any tax withholdings. A freelancer who provided services to multiple clients during a given tax year will receive 1099-MISC forms from each of those clients.

Freelancers are required to pay estimated income taxes to the IRS, in advance and on a quarterly basis, as they have no taxes withheld from their paychecks.

Benefits and Drawbacks of Being a Freelancer

The benefits of being a freelancer include having the freedom to work from home, a flexible work schedule, and a better work-life balance. Freelance work can benefit workers who have been laid off, reducing the incidence of overall unemployment in an economy.

Drawbacks include uncertainty about future income, job stability, and consistency with getting new work. There is also a lack of employer benefits, such as insurance and retirement plans, and sometimes lower per-hour rates compared with employed salary earners. Aside from those who qualify for Pandemic Unemployment Assistance (PUA), freelancers are not eligible for unemployment insurance.

Examples of Freelancers

An example of a freelancer would be an independent journalist who reports on stories of their own choosing and then sells their work to the highest bidder. Another example is a web designer or an app developer who does one-time work for a client and then moves on to another client.

Gig Economy

What Is the Gig Economy?

In a gig economy, temporary, flexible jobs are commonplace and companies tend to hire independent contractors and freelancers instead of full-time employees. A gig economy undermines the traditional economy of full-time workers who often focus on their career development.

Key Takeaways

- The gig economy is based on flexible, temporary, or freelance jobs, often involving connecting with clients or customers through an online platform.

- The gig economy can benefit workers, businesses, and consumers by making work more adaptable to the needs of the moment and demand for flexible lifestyles.

- At the same time, the gig economy can have downsides due to the erosion of traditional economic relationships between workers, businesses, and clients.

Understanding the Gig Economy

In a gig economy, large numbers of people work in part-time or temporary positions or as independent contractors. The result of a gig economy is cheaper, more efficient services, such as Uber or Airbnb, for those willing to use them. People who do not use technological services such as the Internet may be left behind by the benefits of the gig economy. Cities tend to have the most advanced services and are the most entrenched in the gig economy.

A wide variety of positions fall into the category of a gig. The work can range from driving for

Lyft or delivering food to writing code or freelance articles. Adjunct and part-time professors, for example, are contracted employees as opposed to tenure-track or tenured professors. Colleges and universities can cut costs and match professors to their academic needs by hiring more adjunct and part-time professors.

The Factors Behind a Gig Economy

America is well on its way to establishing a gig economy, and estimates show as much as a third of the working population is already in some gig capacity. Experts expect this working number to rise, as these types of positions facilitate independent contracting work, with many of them not requiring a freelancer to come into an office. Gig workers are much more likely to be part-time workers and to work from home.

Employers also have a wider range of applicants to choose from because they do not have to hire someone based on their proximity. Additionally, computers have developed to the point that they can either take the place of the jobs people previously had or allow people to work just as efficiently from home as they could in person.

In the modern digital world, it is becoming increasingly common for people to work remotely or from home. This trend accelerated during the 2020 economic crisis.

Economic reasons also factor into the development of a gig economy. Employers who cannot afford to hire full-time employees to do all the work that needs to be done will often hire part-time or temporary employees to take care of busier times or specific projects.

On the employee's side of the equation, people often find they need to move or take multiple positions to afford the lifestyle they want. It is also common to change careers many times throughout a lifetime, so the gig economy can be viewed as a reflection of this occurring on a large scale.

During 2020, the gig economy experienced significant increases as gig workers have delivered necessities to home-bound consumers, and those whose jobs had been eliminated turned to part-time and contract work for income. Employers will need to plan for changes to the world of work, including the gig economy, when the crisis has ended.

Criticisms of the Gig Economy

Despite its benefits, there are some downsides to the gig economy. While not all employers are inclined to hire contracted employees, the gig economy trend can make it harder for full-time employees to develop in their careers since temporary employees are often cheaper to hire and more flexible in their availability. Workers who prefer a traditional career path and the stability and security that come with it are being crowded out in some industries.

For some workers, the flexibility of working gigs can disrupt the work-life balance, sleep patterns, and activities of daily life. Flexibility in a gig economy often means that workers must make themselves available any time gigs come up, regardless of their other needs, and must always be on the hunt for the next gig. Competition for gigs has increased, too. And unemployment insurance usually doesn't cover gig workers who can't find employment (2020's CARES Act made an exception).

In effect, workers in a gig economy are more like entrepreneurs than traditional workers. While this may mean greater freedom of choice for the individual worker, it also means that the security of a steady job with regular pay, benefits—including a retirement account—and a daily routine that has characterized work for generations are rapidly becoming outdated.

Lastly, because of the fluid nature of gig economy transactions and relationships, long-term relationships between workers, employers, clients, and vendors can erode. This can eliminate the benefits that flow from building long-term trust, customary practice, and familiarity with clients and employers. It could also discourage investment in relationship-specific assets that would otherwise be profitable to pursue since no party has an incentive to invest significantly in a relationship that only lasts until the next gig comes along.

California Assembly Bill 5 (AB5)

What Is California Assembly Bill 5 (AB5)?

California Assembly Bill 5 (AB5), popularly known as the "gig worker bill," is a piece of legislation that went into effect on Jan. 1, 2020, and required companies that hire independent contractors to reclassify them as employees. The passage of Proposition 22 later that year overrode it as far as app-based drivers were concerned.

Key Takeaways

- California Assembly Bill 5 (AB5) extends employee classification status to some gig workers.

- Under AB5, companies must use a three-pronged test to prove workers are independent contractors, not employees.

- AB5 was designed to regulate companies that hire gig workers in large numbers, such as Uber, Lyft, and DoorDash.

- On Sept. 4, 2020, the California legislature passed Assembly Bill 2257, which exempts an extensive list of job categories from AB5 strictures.

- On Nov. 3, 2020, California voters approved Proposition 22, an initiative backed by Uber, Lyft, and DoorDash that legally designates drivers for app-based ride-hailing and delivery services as independent contractors—overriding AB5.

Understanding California Assembly Bill 5 (AB5)

California Assembly Bill 5 (AB5) is a piece of legislation signed into law by Governor Gavin Newsom in September 2019. It went into effect on Jan. 1, 2020 and required companies that hire independent contractors to reclassify them as employees, with a few exceptions. In Sept. 2020, the

California legislature passed Assembly Bill 2257, which rewrote a number of the requirements of AB5 and exempts a substantial list of job categories.

California's AB5 expanded on a ruling made in a case that reached the California Supreme Court in 2018, Dynamex Operations West, Inc. vs. Superior Court of Los Angeles. In the 2018 Dynamex case, the California Supreme Court ruled that companies must use a three-pronged test (known as the ABC test) in determining whether to classify workers as employees or independent contractors. This test assumes that workers are employees unless the company that hires them can prove the following three things:

1. The worker is free to perform services without the control or direction of the company.

2. The worker is performing work tasks that are outside the usual course of the company's business activities.

3. The worker is customarily engaged in an independently established trade, occupation, or business of the same nature as that involved in the work performed.

This test holds companies to a higher standard in proving workers are independent contractors than was previously used in California. AB5 made this test the new gold-standard requirement for all companies in the state. But it was designed to regulate companies that hire gig workers in large numbers, such as Uber, Lyft, and DoorDash.

Uber and Lyft resisted the requirements of AB5, and, on Aug. 10, 2020, California Superior Court Judge Ethan Schulman ordered the companies to reclassify their contract drivers as employees with the same protections and benefits as their other staffers. That entitled them to workers comp, unemployment insurance, paid sick and family leave, and health insurance, among other employee benefits. "To state the obvious, drivers are central, not tangential, to Uber and Lyft's entire ride-hailing business," Judge Schulman wrote. The case was filed by the Attorney General of California, joined by the City Attorneys of Los Angeles, San Diego, and San Francisco.

Gig workers and companies that hire them in other states should pay close attention to AB5. Illinois has considered legislation that mirrors its guidelines. In New York, plans are in the works to introduce legislation that would protect gig workers on a similar scale.

AB5 Impact on Workers

The most immediate implication of AB5 and its one-two-three test is that it turned some independent contractors into employees. "The key factor for gig companies is '2,' which says that anyone performing work for a company that is the same as the business of that company is presumed to be an employee," says Danielle Lackey, chief legal officer at Motus, which provides reimbursement solutions for businesses with mobile-enabled workforces.

Lackey says that, under the bill, if employers begin classifying gig workers as employees, it means these workers will be entitled to a minimum wage, expense reimbursements, health insurance, rest breaks, and the other benefits afforded to employees under California state law. In that sense, the bill creates a level playing field between those working in the gig economy and those hired as regular employees.

There are potential downsides, however—if gig workers who are treated as employees are, because of this, expected to adhere to a new set of standards regarding how they perform their work. For example, one major appeal of being a gig worker is the ability to choose when and when not to work.

Pros

- Creates a level playing field between gig economy workers and those hired as regular employees

- Entitles workers to a minimum wage, employee benefits, and other rewards

Cons

- Potential loss of flexibility regarding hours for reclassified workers

- Reclassifying costs could raise prices for consumers

As an employee, a former gig worker may lose that choice. "Certain people are very attracted to this type of work and flexibility and will most likely drop out, as they may not like fixed schedules or other rules and requirements," says Elliot Dinkin, president and CEO of Cowden Associates, a Pittsburgh-based consulting and actuarial firm.

Lackey says AB5 does not mandate the elimination of flexibility altogether. "But if employers begin incurring the greater cost of paying for employees instead of contractors, they may decide to take advantage of the ability this gives them to exert more control."

AB5 Impact on Businesses

The signing of California AB5 into law affects many, but not all, businesses that rely on gig workers in California. Examples of the types of professions and businesses that are exempt include insurance agents, attorneys, real estate agents, and certain types of business-to-business contractors and referral agencies.1 Companies that are not exempt will have to take a closer look at how they classify employees and independent contractors to ensure that they are not violating the terms of the bill.

For companies that do reclassify gig workers as employees, the question of how easy the transition will be centers on cost. If companies now have to pay a minimum wage, offer paid time off and health insurance, and pay unemployment insurance and worker's compensation benefits for this new crop of employees, that could have a significant impact on the bottom line.

AB5 put ridesharing and delivery companies, such as Uber, Lyft, and DoorDash, in the spotlight. Some analysts suggested that the cost of reclassifying gig workers as employees would potentially bankrupt both companies, destroying the gig worker business model in the process.7 Dinkin says that if companies want to preserve their profit position, then the additional costs of reclassifying will be passed on to the consumers who use their services.

50+

The number of businesses and professions exempted from AB5.

AB2257 Exempts Many Workers From AB5

The controversies surrounding AB5 became so intense that, on Sept. 4, 2020, the California legislature passed—and Governor Gavin Newsom signed—Assembly Bill 2257, which went into effect immediately and rewrote a number of the requirements of AB5.

It exempts an extensive list of job categories from AB5. Among those exempted from the strictures are still and video photographers and editors, freelance writers, content contributors, editors, translators, fine artists, and musicians. One key change was the removal of caps for categories of freelancers that had limited the number of contributions they could make to an outlet, such as a website, without having to be reclassified as employees.

However, workers for gig-economy companies such as Lyft and Uber were not exempted.

A detailed blog post from law firm Seyfarth Shaw LLP noted that AB2257 broadens the business-to-business exemption of AB5, creates an exemption for individual businesspeople who contract with each other, exempts more referral agencies, increases the number of professional exemptions to AB5 (including special provisions for the music industry), and provides wider enforcement powers for district attorneys.

Legal actions that are already underway "may yet affect the scope of AB 2257's application," the Seyfarth post noted. The post's authors also pointed out that—rather than lobby for additional exemptions—companies not covered by AB 2257 "may choose to follow the lead of transportation platform companies, which are funding a ballot initiative (Proposition 22) to create a new class of workers applicable to drivers, if their efforts prove successful."

And those efforts did indeed prove successful on Nov. 3, 2020, when Proposition 22 passed.

Proposition 22 and AB5

As soon as AB5 passed, Uber, Lyft, and DoorDash began to work to unravel it. They responded by heavily supporting California Proposition 22, a ballot initiative that legally designated drivers for app-based ride-hailing and delivery apps as independent contractors. Thanks to their efforts to garner signatures, the measure did get on the ballot in the November 2020 state general election—and was approved, with the support of 58% of California voters.

Prop 22 declares app-based drivers to be independent contractors, not employees—though it does provide certain "engaged time" protections for them, such as healthcare subsidies, and accident and accidental death insurance.

Prop 22 overrode AB5 on the question of whether app-based drivers are employees or independent contractors.

However, on Aug. 20, 2021, Alameda County Superior Court Judge Frank Roesch ruled that two sections of Proposition 22 were unconstitutional and that the measure was unenforceable. Uber and Lyft announced they would appeal, and Prop 22 remains in effect as the court battles continue.

What Is the ABC Test?

The ABC test is a three-pronged test to determine whether to classify workers as employees or independent contractors. It assumes that workers are employees unless the company that hires them can prove the following three things. One, the worker is free to perform services without the control or direction of the company. Two, the worker is performing work tasks that are outside the usual course of the company's business activities. Three, the worker is customarily engaged in an independently established trade, occupation, or business of the same nature as that involved in the work performed.

What Is the Gig Economy?

The gig economy is based on flexible, temporary, or freelance jobs, often involving connecting with clients or customers through an online platform. It can benefit workers, businesses, and consumers by making work more adaptable to the needs of the moment and demand for flexible lifestyles. At the same time, the gig economy can have downsides, due to the erosion of traditional economic relationships between workers, businesses, and clients.

How Does AB5 Impact Workers?

The most immediate implication of AB5 is that it turned some independent contractors into employees. This means these workers will be entitled to a minimum wage, business expense reimbursements, employee benefits, rest breaks, and the other benefits afforded to employees under California state law. However, a gig worker may lose flexibility in choosing when and when not to work.

How Does AB5 Impact Businesses?

It centers on cost. If companies now must pay a minimum wage, offer paid time off and health insurance, and pay unemployment insurance and worker's compensation benefits for this new crop of employees, AB5 could have a significant impact on their bottom line.

5 Challenges for Self-Employed Finance Professionals

How to overcome the unexpected and avoid the pitfalls of going solo

Self-employment is very a universal goal across most industries. While not practical in fields like commercial aviation or nuclear engineering, it is certainly an option for financial professionals.

Many brokers and investment managers understand quite clearly how much of their revenue they must "share" with their employers, and dream of the freedom and income-generating possibilities that go with independence.

Before taking the leap, though, would-be self-employed financial professionals should consider the following five challenges that go with the do-it-yourself approach.

Key Takeaways

- Do not rely on family and friends as clients to help you get started.

- In many cases, taking existing clients to your new firm is forbidden.

- To be successful you will need to be a motivated self-starter—there is nobody else telling you what to do.

- Going solo can be a lonely existence with many late nights.

- Would-be self-employed financial professionals should not underestimate the costs of the resources needed and the time involved to set them up.

1. Friends and Family Aren't Customers

Many would-be solo financial pros build their business plans around the assumption that they will manage the funds of their family and friends and use this as the starting point for their business (and to tide them over). More often, though, this business never materializes and the end result is not only a lot of hard feelings, but a business plan that is undermined at its foundation.

A lot of people are uncomfortable talking about their financial situation with family members or friends, and this cuts both ways in this context. Many entrepreneurs are reluctant to ask their friends and family for business, and just as many (if not more) friends and family members are resistant to give the entrepreneur that level of access and information regarding their personal financial situation.

It's great to have a rich relative who believes in you (it certainly helped Warren Buffett back in the day), or wealthy friends who are willing to help you get started, but these are far and away the exceptions. At best, you may be able to manage a portion of their funds, but you should not expect to feed yourself on the management of the funds of your friends and family.

If nothing else, think about the dinner table at Thanksgiving and how unpleasant that will be if you have lost money for most of the people sitting there.

2. Your Customers Aren't Your Customers

Whatever sort of new investment business you're contemplating (brokerage, investment management, advisory services, etc.) carefully check the provisions of the employment agreement with your current employer, as well as relevant industry, regulatory and association rules regarding the solicitation of existing customers upon switching jobs. In many cases, approaching existing clients of your firm and soliciting them to move their business to you is explicitly forbidden.

It's not unheard of for companies to work out transition agreements with employees who wish to go independent, with the entrepreneur often having to agree to a profit-sharing arrangement. Existing customers can, of course, switch their business to you if they so choose, but you cannot solicit them. Sometimes even informing them of your departure is not allowed.

What that means is that the large business you have built may be off-limits if you wish to venture out on your own—or at least off-limits for a period of time (sometimes measured in years).

Simply going out on your own and poaching customers is a bad idea. For starters, you may be in violation of a contract or civil/securities law in doing so and expose yourself to significant financial consequences. Second, nobody likes poachers—for all the criticism that the financial services industry has taken over the years, it is still a business where reputation counts for a lot and ruining your reputation from the get-go is a sure way to fail.

3. There's No One Else to Push You

There is an image of the independent financial professional as an ambitious and motivated self-starter. That is certainly true, but it only applies to the successful ones.

One of the hardest parts of transitioning to self-employment for many people is also the part that made it so attractive—there is nobody else telling you what to do. If you want to knock off early and go play golf instead of continuing to call prospective clients or work on your marketing pitch, nobody will stop you.

Working as a solo act requires a certain amount of delusional self-confidence, but if you can take it easy early on, just because you know the customers will show up eventually, is an effective way to fail.

4. It Can Be Lonely

It is common to the point of being a cliché to talk about managers and supervisors who live easy off the work done by their subordinates. This is particularly true in Wall Street, where senior analysts and bankers may leave at noon on Friday to play golf. But the first-year employees are stuck in the bowels of the firm assembling pitch books until 11 p.m. on Friday night.

Many new entrepreneurs are surprised to learn just how much work goes into running a business. Much of this is invisible in a large firm with multiple branches—the accounting, HR, legal, compliance and other functions may not even be done on-site or in-country. When it is *your* business, though, it all must get done and by you. This can result in many late nights or weekends spent attending to tasks that are not even why you got into the business in the first place.

This can lead you to become something of a recluse or hermit—not necessarily by choice, but because you must get the work done. If you value a job where you can just "unplug" at 5 or 6 p.m.

every night, going independent may not be for you.

5. You Lose Resources and Brand Name

One of the biggest surprises that independent financial professionals discover is how expensive it is to replicate the resources they are accustomed to when working for a larger firm, such as information sources like Bloomberg and FactSet. While these data sources are invaluable for competing as an independent financial professional, they cost tens of thousands of dollars each year and can represent significant upfront costs for the newly independent professional.

Not only can large firms like Merrill and Edward Jones negotiate more competitive rates for seat licenses, but they have more options in paying for those resources. Not so with the lone independent. There is no negotiating leverage there to speak of, and customers are not going to pay higher fees just because your expenses are harder to leverage. This is also the case when setting up systems for clearing, custody and so on, which can take time.

Expenses like rent, support staff, back-office functions, IT, and info services all add up, and they are not too hard to quantify if you ask the right questions. What can be more challenging, though, is factoring in the cost and value of the reputation of working for a known brand. Think of it this way: If you deal with a "bad rep" at a nationally known firm, there's at least some chance of getting legal and financial satisfaction through the the arbitration process.

Dealing with an independent, though, can bring to mind images of Ponzi schemer Bernie Madoff and the prospect of somebody taking your money and running to the Cayman Islands. That difference in client confidence may be difficult to quantify, but it does show up as a real "cost" when it comes to establishing your own business and your reputation as an independent.

The Bottom Line

Done right—which means careful and detailed planning backed by significant resources to get you through the startup and initial months—working independently can be a great life. There is no shortage of challenges or hassles, but the rewards flow all to you, and you can decide the sort of business you want to operate.

The key is "done right," which means thoroughly understanding not only the requirements and challenges of the business, but your strengths and weaknesses and your ability to respond to both expected and unexpected challenges.

How to Calculate Your Self-Employed Salary

4 steps to help you determine what your skills are worth

Being your own boss is a wonderful feeling, but it also comes with the responsibility of knowing how much to charge for your services. You may enjoy the freedom to take your career in whatever direction most interests you and to decide your own work schedule, dress code, and daily routine. But you also must earn a salary that supports your lifestyle. If you are struggling to figure out what your skills are worth, the following steps will help you set your price.

Key Takeaways

- Between 9.5 million and 44 million Americans are self-employed at least part time.

- To figure out what your skills are worth, start by finding out what others in the same profession charge to get an idea of the average for your field.

- Next, investigate the market for your offerings in your local area and determine what sets you apart from your competition.

- It is essential to tally up the cost of running your business. Overhead expenses such as healthcare, office supplies, and self-employment taxes need to be considered in deciding your salary.

- Do not undervalue your time and expertise; set a salary commensurate with your worth.

A Portrait of the Self-employed

Let us first look at who in the U.S. is self-employed. The exact number is hard to pinpoint, but it falls somewhere between 9.5 million and 44 million. According to the Bureau of Labor Statistics (BLS), approximately 9.5 million Americans are unincorporated self-employed workers.1 The BLS figure, which is derived from household surveys, may under-count total self-employed Americans. One reason: Individuals who work a job for an employer in addition to having a self-employment gig may self-identify as working for an employer if given only one option.

According to the Internal Revenue Service (IRS), there were 19.6 million nonfarm sole proprietorships (unincorporated self-employment businesses) in tax year 2018, based on the number of taxpayers filing a Schedule C. Additionally, the Gig Economy and Self-Employment Report, commissioned by Intuit QuickBooks with research by Gallup and conducted in 2019 (prior to any effects of the 2020 economic crisis on the economy), states that as many as 28% of workers—44 million in total—report being self-employed at some point during a given week. This figure is more likely to include workers who are self-employed part-time as well as employed by an employer.

These industrious people are in a wide range of professions—everything from construction to childcare and professional services to arts and entertainment. Whatever path your self-employment takes, these steps will help you decide how much to charge for your services.

1. Examine Your Peers and Competition

To begin with, check local sources, such as help-wanted ads, advertisements for services, and local business groups or your city's chamber of commerce to get a feel for what other professionals in your field are charging. Trade magazines and national professional organizations are another way to get a feel for your profession's going rate.

Intuit's and Gallup's Gig Economy and Self-Employment Report shows that the median income of workers who are primarily self-employed is $34,751, compared to a median income of $40,800 for those who work for an employer. 4 The total compensation is effectively less because self-employed individuals must pay for their own benefits. However, your self-employment situation depends a lot on your profession.

2. Define Your Local Market

Once you know the average salary for your field, it is time for step two: Investigate the market for your services in your location. Questions you need to answer include:

- Do you live in a large city, where going rates are higher, or in a rural location?

- How much competition do you have in your area?

- Do you offer anything unique or especially desirable that goes beyond your competition?

- Is your field in high demand?

- Are there local networking or business groups you can join to gain contacts and clients?

Once you have answered these questions, you will have a better idea of whom you are competing with, what they are doing, and how you can set yourself apart from the competition. You will also begin to grow your resource of contacts. The bigger your network, the more opportunities there are for your name and business to come up.

3. Tally Your Expenses: Taxes, Healthcare, and Business Expenses

Another common mistake of those new to self-employment is forgetting that freedom is not free. When you're the boss, you need to provide your own healthcare, pay your own taxes, provide for your own vacation time, and keep the lights on, the car full of gas, and the office supply closet stocked. It's also easy to let saving for retirement fall by the wayside, but with no one else to plan for your future, it's crucial that you set aside regular retirement savings.

All this overhead must be considered when deciding your salary. You do not just need to be compensated for your time; you also need to cover your bills.

An app that tracks cash flow and day-to-day business finances, like inDinero or QuickBooks, can make it easy to see how your money comes and goes.

4. Calculate Your Worth

One common mistake of people new to self-employment is undervaluing their time and expertise. Do not fall into that trap—set your price for what you are worth. If you are new to the field, you will need to price yourself at the lower end of the average salary for your field, but if you already have an impressive portfolio or resume, price your work accordingly.

Pricing yourself too low can backfire—potential clients might assume that your low rates mean you lack skill or knowledge. Since you have already determined the average pay of others in your field, you should have a reliable salary range to base your prices on.

Once you have clients, keep track of hours spent on each project. Efficient use of time and impeccable record keeping are necessary for the self-employed. Simplify the record-keeping process with an app that acts as your personal project manager. HoursTracker for iOS or My Work Clock for Android are good choices.

The Bottom Line

When you make the jump to self-employment, you will need to consider several factors before deciding how much to charge potential customers. After considering your profession, your market, and your personal skills and experience, do not forget to look at your costs of doing business. Once you have these numbers established, you will have a better picture of how much to charge and what you will need for a comfortable lifestyle.

Self-Employment Tax

What Is Self-Employment Tax?

Self-employment tax is the imposed tax that a small business owner must pay to the federal government to fund Medicare and Social Security, similar to FICA taxes paid by an employer. Self-employment tax is due when an individual has net earnings of $400 or more in self-employment income over the course of the tax year, or $108.28 or more from a tax-exempt church. Self-employed people who make less than these thresholds from self-employment do not have to pay any tax. Self-employment tax is computed and reported on IRS Form 1040 Schedule SE.

Key Takeaways

- Self-employment tax is imposed to pay for Social Security and Medicare.

- Workers who are considered self-employed include sole proprietors, freelancers, and independent contractors who continue a trade or business.

- Self-employed people who earn less than $400 a year (or less than $108.28 from a church) do not have to pay the tax.

- The CARES Act defers payment of the employer portion of 2020 Social Security taxes to 2021 and 2022.

Understanding Self-Employment Tax

The self-employment tax is to be paid by workers who are considered self-employed. This includes sole proprietors, freelancers, and independent contractors who carry on a trade or business. A member of a partnership that carries on a trade or business may also be self-employed by the Internal Revenue Service. Self-employed individuals must pay self-employment tax as a condition of receiving Social Security benefits upon retirement.

In any business, both the company and the employee are taxed to pay for the two major social welfare programs: Medicare and Social Security. When people are self-employed, in the eyes of the Internal Revenue Service (IRS), they are both the company and the employee, so they pay both portions of this tax.

Social Security tax is assessed at a rate of 6.2% for an employer and 6.2% for the employee. Therefore, a self-employed worker will be taxed 6.2% + 6.2% = 12.4%, as they are both an employer and an employee. The Social Security tax is only applied to the first $137,700 of self-employment income earned, for a maximum tax of $17,074.80 in tax year 2020. For 2021, the maximum income subject to Social Security tax rises to $142,800.

$137,700

The amount of self-employment income above which the portion of self-employment tax that pays for Social Security is no longer levied for the 2020 tax year. (For 2021, the maximum income subject to Social Security tax rises to $142,800.)

Medicare tax is assessed at a rate of 1.45% for an employer and 1.45% for the employee.4 Therefore, a self-employed worker will be taxed 1.45% + 1.45% = 2.9%, as they are both an employer and an employee. The Medicare tax has no upper income limit. Total self-employment tax rate is, therefore, 12.4% + 2.9% = 15.3%.1 A self-employed person having net income of exactly $137,700 in 2020 would have to remit taxes of $21,068.10 = $137,700 * 0.153.

High-income earners face an additional self-employment tax. As a result of the Affordable Care Act (ACA), earnings above $200,000 ($250,000 for married couples filing jointly) are subject to an additional 0.9% Medicare tax.

Self-employment tax is a tax-deductible expense. While the tax is charged on a taxpayer's business profit, the IRS lets them count the "employer" half of the self-employment tax, or 7.65% (calculated as half of 15.3%), as a business deduction for purposes of calculating that taxpayer's income tax.

Example of Self-Employment Tax

Individuals typically pay self-employment tax on 92.35% of their net earnings, not 100%. Robin, who runs a human resources consulting business, calculates their total net income for 2020 to be $200,000 after business expenses have been deducted. Their self-employment tax will be assessed on 92.35% * $200,000 = $184,700. This amount is above the capped limit for the Social Security portion of the self-employment tax. Therefore, Robin's self-employment tax bill will be (12.4% * $137,700 = $17,074.80) + (2.9% * $184,700 = $5,356.30) = $22,431.10.

When Robin files their 2020 income tax return, they can claim an above-the-line deduction for half of their self-employment tax, or $22,431.10 ÷ 2 = $11,215.55. In effect, they get a deduction on the "employer" portion (6.2% Social Security + 1.45% Medicare = 7.65%) of their self-employment tax.

Special Considerations

Workers who are self-employed aren't subject to withholding tax, but the IRS requires taxpayers to make quarterly estimated tax payments in order to cover their self-employment tax obligation, in addition to their federal and state income tax obligation.8 However, the CARES (Coronavirus Aid, Relief, and Economic Security) Act, signed into law by the president on March 27, 2020, defers payment of the employer portion of self-employment taxes attributable to Social Security for the period of March 27, 2020, through Dec. 31, 2020. It defers payment of 50% of those taxes until Dec. 31, 2021, and the other 50% until Dec. 31, 2022.

Self-Employed Contributions Act (SECA) Tax

What Is the Self-Employed Contributions Act (SECA) Tax?

The Self-Employed Contributions Act (SECA) tax is a levy from the U.S. government on those who work for themselves, rather than for an outside company. It requires self-employed workers to contribute tax equivalent to both the employer and employee portions of the Federal Insurance Contributions Act (FICA) tax, which funds Social Security and Medicare.

Key Takeaways

- SECA requires self-employed individuals to pay into the Social Security and Medicare tax funds.

- As self-employed individuals are their own employers, they are permitted to deduct the employer-portion of SECA taxes as a business expense.

- Net self-employment earnings of less than $400 do not incur a SECA tax.

Understanding the Self-Employed Contributions Act (SECA) Tax

SECA taxes are computed based on net earnings, defined as the gross income derived from business activities, minus the expenses incurred while doing business.

Social Security tax is assessed at a basic rate of 6.2% for an employer and 6.2% for the employee. Self-employed taxpayers subject to SECA are taxed at 12.4% (6.2% + 6.2%), as they are both employer and employee.

There are limits, however, on how much income is subject to this percentage. The Social Security tax is only applied to the first $137,700 of net income, for a maximum tax of $17,075 in tax year 2020. (In 2021, the tax will be applied to the first $142,800 of net income, for a maximum tax of $17,707.)4 Any income above that level is not subject to Social Security tax.

The Medicare tax rate is 2.9% (1.45% for employers plus 1.45% for employees), and there is no exemption above a certain income. Total SECA tax is, therefore, 15.3%.3 A self-employed person who has a net income of exactly $137,700 in 2020 would have to remit SECA taxes of 15.3% of their income (12.4% + 2.9%), which comes to $21,068 (in 2021, 15.3% of net income of $142,800 would be $21,848 in SECA taxes).

Unless there is a specific agreement in place between countries, expatriates (Americans who live and work abroad) are still expected to pay SECA taxes on earnings that are gained in the process of being self-employed.

High-income earners face an additional SECA levy. As a result of the Affordable Care Act (ACA), individuals with net income above $200,000 ($250,000 for married couples filing jointly) will be subject to an additional 0.9% Medicare tax.

Deducting the Self-Employed Contributions Act (SECA) Tax

The employer portion of the payment is deductible as a business expense. In other words, the IRS allows self-employed individuals to use the employer half of the self-employment tax as a business deduction for purposes of calculating the taxpayer's income tax. This considers that the efforts of running a company are taken on by an individual, rather than an "employer," which would be the case for an employee of a company.

It is important to note that self-employment taxes refer to Social Security and Medicare taxes, like FICA taxes paid by an employer. When a taxpayer takes a deduction of one-half of the SECA tax, it is only a deduction for the calculation of that taxpayer's income tax. It does not reduce the net earnings from self-employment or reduce the self-employment tax itself.

Paying the Self-Employed Contributions Act (SECA) Tax

Since taxpayers who are self-employed aren't subject to withholding tax, the IRS requires SECA tax to be included in quarterly estimated payments of income taxes. If self-employed net earnings are less than $400 (or $108.28 from a church or other qualified church-controlled organization exempt from employer Social Security and Medicare taxes), no SECA tax is due, and it is not required to be listed on a tax return. However, if self-employed net earnings are above this minimum, SECA tax must be paid on the entire amount, including the amount under the minimum.

15 Tax Deductions and Benefits for the Self-Employed

Know where you can save money and grow your profits

Throughout the years, legislators have written numerous lines into the tax code to soften the blow of the extra costs that self-employed persons must shoulder as they do business. The Tax Cuts and Jobs Act (TCJA), passed in December 2017 and effective as of the 2018 tax year, made several changes to self-employed tax deductions. Many of these changes are temporary and set to expire in 2025, but others are permanent.

The law affects small businesses in many ways, particularly via a 20% qualified business income deduction for pass-through businesses—those that pay taxes through individual taxpayer(s) rather than through a corporation.

Some deductions that have been eliminated include:

- Entertainment and fringe benefit deduction

- Employees' parking, mass transit, or commuting expenses deduction

- Domestic production activities deduction

- Local lobbying expenses deduction

- Deduction of settlement or legal fees in a sexual harassment case, when the settlement is subject to a nondisclosure

A review of the most common self-employed taxes and deductions is necessary to keep you up to date on any necessary changes to your quarterly estimated tax payments.

Key Takeaways

- The Tax Cuts and Jobs Act, which went into effect in 2018, included a number of changes to tax deductions for the self-employed.

- If you are self-employed, it is important to review what you are allowed to deduct each year to make your business as profitable as possible.

- There are two ways of calculating a deduction for a home office and a vehicle used for business purposes. It pays to do calculations for both methods to see which is more financially beneficial.

- Meals with clients and business travel are deductible, but meals that are included with entertainment may not be, according to the TCJA.

- Premiums for insurance that you buy to protect your business and for health insurance are legitimate deductions. And do not forget startup, advertising, and retirement-plan costs.

1. Self-Employment Tax

The self-employment tax refers to the Medicare and Social Security taxes that self-employed people must pay. This includes freelancers, independent contractors, and small-business owners. The self-employment tax rate is 15.3%, which includes 12.4% for Social Security and 2.9% for Medicare.

Employers and employees share the self-employment tax. Each pays 7.65%. People who are fully self-employed pay the total themselves.

An additional 0.9% Medicare tax rate applies if income is above a certain threshold amount. The threshold figures are:

- Married filing jointly: $250,000

- Married filing separate: $125,000

- Single: $200,000

- Head of household: (with qualifying person): $200,000

- Qualifying widow(er) with dependent child: $200,0006

The income thresholds for additional Medicare tax apply not just to self-employment income but to your combined wages, compensation, and self-employment income. So if you have $100,000 in self-employment income and your spouse has $160,000 in employee wages, you'll have to pay the additional Medicare tax of 0.9% on the $10,000 by which your joint income exceeds the $250,000 threshold.

Paying extra taxes to be your own boss is no fun. The good news is that the self-employment tax will cost you less than you might think because you get to deduct half of your self-employment tax from your net income when calculating your income tax. The IRS treats the "employer" portion of the self-employment tax as a business expense and allows you to deduct it accordingly.

It is important to note that the self-employment tax refers to Social Security and Medicare taxes, similar to FICA paid by an employer. When a taxpayer takes a deduction of one-half of the self-employment tax, it is only a deduction for the calculation of that taxpayer's income tax. It does not reduce the net earnings from self-employment or reduce the self-employment tax itself.

Remember, you are paying the first 7.65% whether you are self-employed or work for someone else. And when you work for someone else, you are indirectly paying the employer portion because that's money your employer cannot afford to add to your salary.

Self-employed individuals determine their net income from self-employment and deductions based on their method of accounting. Most self-employed individuals use the cash method of accounting and will therefore include all income actually or constructively received during the period and all deductions actually paid during the period when determining their net income from self-employment.

2. Home Office

The home office deduction is one of the more complex of all. In short, the cost of any workspace you use regularly and exclusively for your business, regardless of whether you rent or own it, can be deducted as a home office expense.

You are basically on the honor system, but you should be prepared to defend your deduction in the event of an IRS audit. One way to do this is to prepare a diagram of your workspace, with accurate measurements, in case you are required to submit this information to substantiate your deduction, which uses the square footage of your workspace in its calculation.

In addition to the office space itself, the expenses you can deduct for your home office include the business percentage of deductible mortgage interest, home depreciation, utilities, homeowners insurance, and repairs that you pay during the year.

If your home office occupies 15% of your home, for example, then 15% of your annual electricity bill becomes tax-deductible. Some of these deductions, such as mortgage interest and home depreciation, apply only to those who own rather than rent their home office space.

How to Calculate the Home Office Deduction

You have two choices for calculating your home office deduction: the standard method or the simplified option, and you do not have to use the same method every year. The standard method requires you to calculate your actual home office expenses and keep detailed records in the event of an audit.

The simplified option lets you multiply an IRS-determined rate by your home office square footage. To use the simplified option, your home office must not be larger than 300 square feet and you cannot deduct depreciation or home-related itemized deductions.

The simplified option is an obvious choice if you are pressed for time or cannot pull together good records of your deductible home office expenses. However, because the simplified option is calculated as $5 per square foot, with a maximum of 300 square feet, the most you will be able to deduct is $1,500.

If you want to make sure you are claiming the largest home office deduction you are entitled to, you will want to calculate the deduction using both the regular and simplified methods. If you choose the standard method, calculate the deduction using IRS form 8829, Expenses for Business Use of Your Home.

3. Internet and Phone Bills

Regardless of whether you claim the home office deduction, you can deduct the business portion of your phone, fax, and internet expenses. The key is to deduct only the expenses related to your business. For example, you could deduct the internet-related costs of running a website for your business.

If you have just one phone line, you should not deduct your entire monthly bill, which includes both personal and business use. According to the IRS website, "You can't deduct the cost of basic local telephone service (including any taxes) for the first telephone line you have in your home, even if you have an office in your home."11 However, you can deduct 100% of the additional cost of long-distance business calls or the cost of a second phone line dedicated solely to your business.

4. Health Insurance Premiums

If you are self-employed, pay for your own health insurance premiums, and are not eligible to participate in a plan through your spouse's employer, you can deduct all of your health, dental, and qualified long-term care (LTC) insurance premiums.

You can also deduct premiums that you paid to provide coverage for your spouse, your dependents, and your children who were younger than 27 at year-end, even if they are not dependents on your taxes. Calculate the deduction using the Self-Employed Health Insurance Deduction Worksheet in IRS publication 535.

5. Meals

A meal is a tax-deductible business expense when you are traveling for business, at a business conference, or entertaining a client. The meal cannot be lavish or extravagant under the circumstances, and in the past, you could only deduct 50% of the meal's actual cost if you keep your receipts, or 50% of the standard meal allowance if you keep records of the time, place, and business purpose of your travel but not your actual meal receipts.

However, the deduction has been amended, according to the Consolidated Appropriations Act, 2021, H.R. 133, Temporary allowance of a full deduction for business meals. The bill temporarily allows a 100% business expense deduction for meals (rather than the current 50%) if the expense is for food or beverages provided by a restaurant. This provision is effective for expenses incurred after Dec. 31, 2020, and expires at the end of 2022.

The standard meal allowance is the federal M&IE rate, found on the U.S. General Services Administration (GSA) website for each tax year. The lunch you eat alone at your desk is not tax-deductible.

Additionally, prior to the Tax Cuts and Jobs Act, meals and entertainment expenses were considered in unison. For tax years 2018 and later, according to the IRS website, "if food or beverages are provided during or at an entertainment event, and the food and beverages were purchased separately from the entertainment or the cost of the food and beverages was stated separately from the cost of the entertainment on one or more bills, invoices, or receipts, you may be able to deduct the separately stated costs as a meal expense."13 However, if the meals are not separately identified on the receipt, they cannot be deducted at all.

6. Travel

To qualify as a tax deduction, business travel must last longer than an ordinary workday, require you to get sleep or rest, and take place away from the general area of your tax home (usually, outside the city where your business is located).

Handing out business cards during your friend's bachelor party in Vegas does not make your trip tax-deductible.

Further, to be considered a business trip, you should have a specific business purpose planned before you leave home and you must engage in business activity—such as finding new customers, meeting with clients, or learning new skills related to your business—while you are on the road. Handing out business cards at a bar during your friend's bachelor party will not make your trip to Vegas tax-deductible.

Keep complete and accurate records and receipts for your business travel expenses and activities, as this deduction often draws scrutiny from the IRS.

Deductible travel expenses include the cost of transportation to and from your destination (such as plane fare), the cost of transportation at your destination (such as car rental, Uber fare, or subway tickets), lodging, and meals.

You cannot deduct lavish or extravagant expenses, but you do not have to choose the cheapest options available, either. Do not forget that you, not your fellow taxpayers, will be paying the bulk of your travel costs, so it is in your interest to keep them reasonable.

Your travel expenses for business are 100% deductible, except for meals, which are limited to 50%.[14] If your trip combines business with pleasure, things get a lot more complicated; in a nutshell, you can only deduct the expenses related to the business portion of your trip.

If your spouse (who does not work for you as an employee) joins you on a business trip, for example, you can only deduct the portion of lodging and transportation costs that would have been incurred if you had traveled alone. Do not forget that the business part of your trip also needs to be planned ahead.

7. Vehicle Use

When you use your car for business, your expenses for those drives are tax-deductible. Make sure to keep excellent records of the date, mileage, and purpose for each trip, and do not try to claim personal car trips as business car trips.

You can calculate your deduction using either the standard mileage rate determined annually by the IRS or your actual expenses.

The standard mileage rates are 57.5 cents per mile in 2020 and 56 cents per mile in 2021.[151613]

Using the standard mileage rate is easiest because it requires minimal record-keeping and calculation. Just write down the business miles you drive and the dates you drive them. Then, multiply your total annual business miles by the standard mileage rate. This amount is your deductible expense.

To use the actual expense method, you must calculate the percentage of driving you did for business all year as well as the total cost of operating your car, including depreciation, gas, oil changes, registration fees, repairs, and car insurance. If you spent $3,000 on car operating expenses and used your car for business 10% of the time, your deduction would be $300.

If you want to use the standard mileage rate on a car you own, you need to use that method in the first year the car is available for use in your business. In later years, you can choose to use either the standard mileage rate or switch to actual expenses. If you are leasing a vehicle and wish to use the standard mileage rate, you must use the standard mileage rate in each year of the lease period.

As with the home office deduction, it may be worth calculating your deduction both ways so you can claim the larger amount.

8. Interest

Interest on a business loan from a bank is a tax-deductible business expense. If a loan is used for both business and personal purposes, the business portion of the loan's interest expense is allocated based on the allocation of the loan's proceeds.

You will need to track the disbursement of funds for various uses if the entire loan is not used for business-related activities. Credit card interest is not tax-deductible when you incur the interest for personal purchases, but when the interest applies to business purchases, it is tax-deductible.

That said, it's always cheaper to spend only the money you already have and not incur any interest expenses at all. A tax deduction only gives you some of your money back, not all of it, so try to avoid borrowing money. For some businesses, though, borrowing may be the only way to get up and running, to sustain the business through slow periods, or to ramp up for busy periods.

9. Publications and Subscriptions

The cost of specialized magazines, journals, and books related to your business is tax-deductible. A daily newspaper, for example, would not be specific enough to be considered a business expense. A subscription to "Nation's Restaurant News" would be tax-deductible if you are a restaurant owner, and Nathan Myhrvold's several-hundred-dollar "Modernist Cuisine" boxed set is a legitimate book purchase for a self-employed, high-end personal chef.

10. Education

Any education expenses you want to deduct must be related to maintaining or improving your skills for your existing business. The cost of classes to prepare for a new line of work is not deductible.

If you're a real estate consultant, taking a course called "Real Estate Investment Analysis" to brush up on your skills would be tax-deductible, but a class on how to teach yoga would not be.

11. Business Insurance

Do you pay premiums for any type of insurance to protect your business, such as fire insurance, credit insurance, car insurance on a business vehicle, or business liability insurance? If so, you can deduct your premiums.

Some people do not like paying insurance premiums because they perceive them as a waste of money if they never have to file a claim. The business insurance tax deduction can help ease that dislike.

12. Rent

If you rent out an office space, you can deduct the amount you pay for rent. You can also deduct amounts paid for any equipment you rent. And if you must pay a fee to cancel a business lease, that expense is deductible, too.

But you cannot deduct rent expenses on any property that you own, even partially. Also, rent must be reasonable in amount. The need for a reasonableness test typically arises when you and the owner are related, but rent is considered reasonable if it were the same amount you would pay to a stranger.

13. Startup Costs

The IRS usually requires you to deduct major expenses over time as capital expenses rather than all at once. However, you can deduct up to $5,000 in business startup costs in the first year of active trade or business.

Examples of tax-deductible startup costs include market research and travel-related costs for starting your business, scoping out potential business locations, advertising, attorney fees, and accountant fees.

The $5,000 deduction is reduced by the amount your total startup cost exceeds $50,000. If you set up a corporation or LLC for your business, you can deduct up to $5,000 more in organizational costs such as state filing fees and legal fees.

Professional fees to consultants, attorneys, accountants, and the like are also deductible at any time, even if they are not startup costs.

Business expenses such as buying equipment or vehicles aren't considered startup costs, but they can be depreciated or amortized as capital expenditures.

SEP Account: Jessica Perez

14. Advertising

Do you pay for ads on Facebook or Google ads, a billboard, a TV commercial, or mailed flyers? The costs you incur to advertise your business are tax-deductible.

You can even deduct the cost of advertising that encourages people to donate to charity while also putting your business' name before the public in the hope of gaining customers. A sign advertising "Holiday Toy Drive sponsored by Robert's Hot Dogs," for example, would be tax-deductible.

15. Retirement Plan Contributions

One deduction you can take going into business for yourself that is especially worthwhile is the deduction for self-employed retirement plan contributions. Contributions to SEP-IRAs, SIMPLE IRAs, and solo 401(k)s reduce your tax bill now and help you rack up tax-deferred investment gains for later.

For the 2020 and 2021 tax year, for example, you could feasibly contribute as much as $19,500 in deferred salary (or $26,000, with the $6,500 catch-up contribution, if you're 50 or older).

Plus, you can contribute another 25% of your net self-employment earnings after deducting one-half of self-employment tax and contributions for yourself. The total maximum contributions cannot exceed $57,000 for 2020 and $58,000 for 2021 (not counting catch-up contributions of $6,500, if eligible) for both contribution categories, with a self-employed 401(k).

Contribution limits vary by plan type and the IRS adjusts the maximums annually. Of course, you cannot contribute more than you earn, and this benefit will only help you if you have enough profits to take advantage of it.

The Bottom Line

Most small business tax deductions are more complicated than this brief overview describes—it is the U.S. Tax Code, after all—but now you have a good introduction to the basics.

There are more deductions available than those listed here, but these are some of the biggest ones. Office supplies, credit card processing fees, tax preparation fees, and repairs and maintenance for business property and equipment are also deductible.

Still, other business expenses can be depreciated or amortized, meaning you can deduct a small amount of the cost each year over several years.

Remember, any time you are not sure whether a cost is a legitimate business expense, ask yourself, "Is this an ordinary and necessary expense in my line of work?" This is the same question the IRS will ask when examining your deductions if you are audited. If the answer is no, do not take the deduction.

And if you are not sure, seek professional help with your business tax return from a certified public accountant (CPA).

7 Insurance-Based Tax Deductions You May Be Missing

See if you qualify for any of them

When it comes to filing taxes, getting the lowest tax liability is not all about skill—it's about what you know. Unfortunately, many taxpayers miss deductions and credits simply because they are not aware of them. Several of the most overlooked deductions pertain to health and medical expenses, as well as to insurance premiums.

The 2017 Tax Cuts and Jobs Act (TCJA) eliminated many deductions, but it left most of the ones discussed below unchanged.

Key Takeaways

- Many missed deductions are related to insurance premiums, medical expenses, and other health-related costs.

- Disability insurance is an important but complicated tax deduction.

- Health Savings Account (HSA) contributions are tax-free up to a predetermined cap.

- Life insurance and business-related insurance premiums also may qualify.

1. Disability Insurance

Disability insurance is the most common type of premium that is overlooked as a tax deduction. This type of insurance can provide supplemental income if you are disabled and cannot work. The deductibility of these premiums, however, is complicated and limited.

The Internal Revenue Service (IRS) permits self-employed taxpayers to deduct "overhead insurance that pays for business overhead expenses you have during long periods of disability caused by your injury or sickness." But "you can't deduct premiums for a policy that pays for lost earnings due to sickness or disability."

The only disability insurance that is eligible for deduction is the kind that covers business overhead expenses while you are out on leave. This type of insurance would cover items such as rent and utilities that are unavoidable for the duration of disability leave.

If you deduct the premium, then any proceeds paid from the policy will be considered taxable income. By contrast, policy benefits will not be taxable if you pay for the premium yourself and do not deduct the premium—an arrangement used by some taxpayers so that they can receive tax-free benefits to cover business overhead expenses if they become disabled. Proceeds are also taxable if your employer paid for your disability insurance, rather than if you bought it yourself with your own after-tax dollars.

There are several rules to follow if you deduct health insurance expenses, based on your employment status, whether you itemize deductions, and whether you have paid your premiums using pre- or post-tax dollars.

2. Health Savings Accounts

Another insurance-related tax perk that people without access to traditional group health coverage should be aware of is a Health Savings Account (HSA), which combines a tax-advantaged savings element with a high-deductible health insurance policy.

All HSA contributions, up to the maximum permitted by law, are tax-deductible, even for those who do not itemize on Schedule C. For the 2020 tax year, you can contribute up to $3,550 ($3,600 in 2021) if you have a single coverage plan or $7,100 ($7,200 in 2021) if you have a family plan—with an additional $1,000 contribution allowed for taxpayers over the age of 55.4

Employers can also make contributions to an HSA on behalf of employees, like a 401(k). However, the sum of employer and employee contributions cannot exceed the annual contribution limit for each coverage type.

Health Savings Accounts can yield a triple tax benefit in the form of tax-deductible contributions, tax-deferred growth, and tax-free withdrawals when funds are used to pay for qualified medical expenses.

3. Medical Expenses

Medical expenses are deductible but only in the amount that they surpass a certain percentage of the taxpayer's adjusted gross income (AGI). That percentage keeps changing due to various legislation (most recently ranging from 7.5% to 10%), but it always stays high enough to keep most people from qualifying. The percentage is 7.5% of your AGI for the 2020 and 2021 tax years.

If you have substantial medical bills pending, then you can boost your deduction by scheduling other medical procedures or expenses in the same year. One caveat is that if you get a reimbursement check the following year from your insurance company, then you will have to declare the amount of the deduction that was reimbursed as income the following year.

For example, if you deducted $17,000 for surgery in one year and your insurance company sent you a $10,000 check for the surgery the next year, then that amount would have to be declared as income in the year when the check arrives.

If there is a chance that you may get medical expenses covered by your insurance company in the future, then do not declare this deduction. You can always submit an amended return for the year when you would have received the deduction if your insurance claim is denied.

4. Unemployment/Workers' Compensation

It is important to distinguish unemployment compensation paid through a state unemployment agency from workers' compensation, which is awarded to workers who cannot perform their duties as a result of an injury.

Unemployment benefits are always taxable, as they are considered a replacement for regular earned income. You will receive a Form 1099-G listing the total unemployment compensation you received throughout the year, and this amount should be reported on IRS Form 1040. Workers' compensation benefits that you receive should not be declared as income. This also includes survivor's benefits.

5. Deductions for the Self-Employed

Self-employed taxpayers and other business entities can deduct business-related insurance premiums, including health and dental insurance premiums, as well as long-term care premiums. Vehicle insurance can also be deducted if the taxpayer elected to report actual expenses and is not taking the standard mileage rate.

Be sure to keep documentation of all premiums paid toward eligible insurance expenses, as well as any other deductible expenses that you plan to claim, such as computer equipment or a home office.

6. Other Qualifying Plans

Qualified plans are not the only type of retirement savings vehicle that can be funded with tax-deductible premiums; 412(i) plans are also tax-deferred. This defined-benefit plan can provide substantial deductions for small-business owners looking to catch up on their retirement savings and receive a guaranteed income stream in the future.

A 412(i) plan is funded solely with insurance products such as cash value life insurance or fixed annuity contracts, and the plan owner can deduct up to hundreds of thousands of dollars in contributions to this plan every year.

Participants in standard qualified plans, such as 401(k) plans through an employer, can purchase a limited amount of either term or permanent life insurance coverage, subject to specific restrictions. But the coverage must be considered "incidental" according to IRS regulations. According to the IRS, an insurance policy is "incidental" if "less than 50 percent of the employer contribution credited to each participant's account is used to purchase ordinary life insurance policies on the participant's life."

Life insurance death benefits paid out of qualified plans enjoy tax-free status, and this insurance can be used to pay the taxes on the plan proceeds that must be distributed when the participant dies.14

7. Are Life Insurance Premiums Tax-Deductible?

Life insurance can help you provide a measure of family security for your loved ones if something should happen to you. You may be wondering whether life insurance premiums are deductible on your personal tax return, and the answer is no. But premiums are deductible as a business-related expense (if the insured is an employee or a corporate officer of the company, and if the company is not a direct or indirect beneficiary of the policy).

The death benefit is tax-free for individual policy owners and their beneficiaries.

Although death benefits for business-related beneficiaries are often tax-free as well, there are certain situations in which the death benefit for corporate-owned life insurance can be taxable. However, employers offering group term life coverage to employees can deduct premiums that they pay on the first $50,000 of benefits per employee, and amounts up to this limit are not counted as income to the employees.

Life insurance premiums can also often be deducted for most types of non-qualified plans, such as deferred compensation or executive bonuses. Usually, the premiums are considered compensation for key executives under the rules of these plans. However, in some cases, the deduction cannot be taken until the employee constructively receives the benefit.

The Bottom Line

These are only a few of the commonly overlooked deductions and tax benefits related to insurance for which business and individual taxpayers are eligible. Other deductions relating to compensation, production, and depreciation of buildings and equipment are listed on the IRS website. Talking to your accountant or other tax professional can help you determine which tax deductions related to insurance you are eligible to claim to help minimize what you owe.

7 Ways to Avoid Self-Employed Tax Penalties

Tips to help you stay out of trouble with the IRS

People who are self-employed are required to send in quarterly estimated tax payments since tax is not withheld from their wages as it is for employees. But if your income varies from month to month or year to year, it is tough to determine the amount to pay. You don't want to send in so much that you can't meet other expenses, or so little that you get slapped with a shocking tax bill at tax return time—not to mention underpayment penalties.

The following tips will help you calculate your quarterly estimated tax payments to minimize your chances of incurring penalties or breaking your budget.

Key Takeaways

- Open separate checking and credit card accounts for your business. This will provide you with an easy reference for your business expenses and income.

- File your quarterly payments and, if anything, overpay a little. You will get it back.

- The first year, get advice from a self-employed friend, an accountant, or the IRS helpline.

Due to Hurricane Ida, some residents and business owners in Louisiana and parts of Mississippi, New York, and New Jersey have been granted extensions on their deadlines for filings and payments to the IRS. Most relate to upcoming due dates for quarterly filings and payments. For details, go to the IRS "Tax Relief in Disaster Situations" page and click on "2021."

to the IRS. Most relate to upcoming due dates for quarterly filings and payments. For details, go to the IRS "Tax Relief in Disaster Situations" page and click on "2021."

1. Base Your Payments on Last Year's Earnings

You can avoid paying a penalty by paying at least the same amount in taxes as you did the previous year if you were self-employed then as well. You can find the total taxes you paid on last year's tax return. Just divide last year's taxes into four equal payments and send each of them in by the IRS' quarterly due dates: April 15, June 15, Sept. 15, and Jan. 15.

If your taxes turn out to be higher this year than last, you will still be liable for what you owe but you will not have to pay an underpayment penalty as well. Let us say, for example, you paid $4,000 in taxes last year. You send in four equal payments of $1,000 this year. You calculate your taxes at the end of this year to be $5,500. You can send the IRS a check at tax time for the $1,500 difference without paying a penalty.

You should note that if you had no tax liability in the prior year, you won't incur a penalty for not making any payments before tax return time. You can choose how much to send in throughout the year but be aware that you could have a large tax bill at the end of the year if you do not send in enough.

2. Get Advice the First Year

During the first year of self-employment, talk to a friend who is self-employed or hire an accountant to handle your tax calculations for you. Either way, you can figure out how much to pay, determine what expenses you can deduct, and get comfortable with the process.

3. Use Separate Accounts for Business Expenses

It will simplify your life and make it easier to estimate your quarterly taxes if you open a separate bank account and a credit card account reserved for business expenses only.

These provide records of your business expenses for easy reference come tax time. It is much simpler than wading through a pile of paper receipts when you are doing your taxes, and it is much easier to check back through if a question about expenses comes up.

4. Keep a Running Tally of Your Income

You could get sticker shock next April if you do not keep a running tally of your income and pay your estimated tax accordingly. Calculate your income at the end of each quarter and use this as a basis for whether you should increase or lower your quarterly payments.

If you use that dedicated checking account for your business income deposits, a running tally will take a couple of minutes to check in your online bank records.

5. Use the IRS 1040-ES Worksheet

If your income varies widely from year to year, the best way to estimate your quarterly payments is to use the 1040-ES worksheet from the IRS.6 The worksheet guides you through calculating your expected tax liability and takes into account certain common deductions you may qualify to claim.

You can fill out the worksheet every quarter, or at least every quarter that represents an unusual change in your income. If your business experiences a significant amount of variation from quarter to quarter, you will need to adjust your estimated tax payment to avoid a shocking surprise next April.

6. Always Overestimate, at Least a Little

Tax penalties can be pricey, depending on how much you underestimated your taxes due. There is a fine for falling short, around .5% of the amount owed for each month or part of a month the tax is not paid.7 Also, interest is charged on the amount you underpay from the day your quarterly payment is due until the day it is paid.

The interest rate for individual taxpayers, based on the federal short-term funds rate plus three percentage points, is set each quarter by the IRS.8 So, if you underpay for the first quarter of a tax year, you could owe a different penalty amount than if you underpay for the third quarter.

For Q4 2021, the interest rate on underpayments by individual taxpayers amounts to 3%.

If you are unsure of the exact amount to pay each quarter, slightly overestimate your taxes. You will not lose any money in the long term. You will just get it back as a tax refund.

7. Put the IRS Tax Help Line on Speed Dial

The IRS's free helpline is your best source for answering any question you may have. The number for individual taxpayers is 800-829-1040.

Unless you hire someone to do your taxes for you, you are your own accounting department. Unless you are an accountant, you may very well have some questions, at least during the first year of self-employment.

The Bottom Line

If you are self-employed, you need to be incredibly careful when calculating and paying your estimated taxes in order not to incur underpayment penalties. If you follow the tips above for calculating your quarterly estimated tax payments, you can minimize your chances of incurring fines and interest—without breaking your budget. Always consult with a tax advisor if you have questions relating to your specific tax situation.

How to Build Your Own Retirement Plan

Strategies for saving when you're self-employed

The joys of self-employment are many, but so are the stressors. High among those is the need to plan for retirement entirely on your own. You oversee creating a satisfying quality of life post-retirement. When it comes to building that life, the earlier you start, the better. Luckily, there are several retirement plans for those who are self-employed.

Key Takeaways

- For self-employed workers, setting up a retirement plan is a do-it-yourself job.

- There are four available plans tailored for the self-employed: one-participant 401(k), SEP IRA, SIMPLE IRA, and Keogh plan.

- Health savings plans (HSAs) and traditional and Roth IRAs are two more supplemental options.

Growth in Self-Employment

A 2019 study conducted by the Freelancers Union and Upwork estimates that there are 57 million freelancers in the U.S., an increase from 53 million reported in 2014. According to the report, this represents more than 35% of the country's entire workforce.1

While this entrepreneurial spirit is to be applauded, less laudable is the fact that 30% of those who are self-employed save for retirement sporadically while 15% aren't even saving at all. That is a problem. If you are self-employed, you are busy, but retirement savings must be a priority.

Why Saving Is Hard for the Self-Employed

The reasons for not saving toward retirement will not be a surprise to any self-employed person. The most common include:

- the lack of steady income

- paying off major debts

- health care expenses

- education expenses

- costs of running the business2

Setting up a retirement plan is a do-it-yourself job just like everything else an entrepreneur undertakes. No human resources (HR) staffer is going to walk you through the company-sponsored 401(k) plan application. There are no matching contributions, no shares of company stock, and no automatic payroll deductions.

You will have to be highly disciplined in contributing to the plan and, because the amount you can put in your retirement accounts depends on how much you earn, you will not really know until the end of the year how much you can contribute.

Still, if freelancers have unique challenges when it comes to saving for retirement, they have unique opportunities, too. Funding your retirement account can be considered part of your business expenses, as is any time or money you spend on establishing and administering the plan. Even more important, a retirement account allows you to make pretax contributions, which lowers your taxable income.

Many retirement plans for the self-employed allow you, as a business owner, to contribute more money annually than you could to an individual IRA.

Self-Employed Retirement Saving Plans

There are four retirement savings options favored by the self-employed. Some are single-player 401(k) plans, while others are based on individual retirement accounts (IRAs). They are:

- One-participant 401(k)

- SEP IRA

- SIMPLE IRA

- Keogh plan3

With all four of these options, your contributions are tax deductible, and you will not pay taxes as they grow over the years (until you cash out at retirement). Their complexity and suitability vary, depending on the size of your business, both in terms of personnel and earnings. Let us look at each in more depth.

To avoid penalties with any of these plans, you will need to leave your savings in the account until you are 59½ although there are certain hardship exemptions.

One-Participant 401(k)

A one-participant 401(k), as it's officially dubbed by the IRS, also goes by the names solo 401(k), solo-k, uni-k, or individual 401(k). It is reserved for sole proprietors with no employees, other than a spouse working for the business.

How it Works

The one-participant plan closely mirrors the 401(k)s offered by many larger companies, down to the amounts you can contribute each year. The significant difference is that you get to contribute as the employee and the employer, giving you a higher limit than many other tax-advantaged plans.

So if you participate in a standard corporate 401(k), you would make investments as a pretax payroll deduction from your paycheck, and your employer has the option of matching those contributions up to certain amounts. You get a tax break for your contribution, and the employer gets a tax break for its match. With a one-participant 401(k) plan, you can contribute to each capacity, as an employee (called an elective deferral) and as a business owner (an employee non-elective contribution).

Elective deferrals for 2021 can be up to $19,500, or $26,000 if age 50 or older. Total contributions to the plan cannot exceed $58,000, or $64,000 for people age 50 or older as of 2021. If your spouse works for you, they can also make contributions up to the same amount, and then you can match those. So, you see why the solo 401(k) offers the most generous contribution limits of the plans.

Setting it Up

Some paperwork is required, but it is not too onerous. To establish an individual 401(k), a business owner has to work with a financial institution, which may impose fees and limits as to what investments are available in the plan. Some plans may limit you to a fixed list of mutual funds, but a little bit of shopping will turn up many reputable and well-known firms that offer low-cost plans with a great deal of flexibility.

"Generally, 401(k)s are complex plans, with significant accounting, administration, and filing requirements," says James B. Twining, CFP, founder, and wealth manager of Financial Plan.7 "However, a solo 401(k) is quite simple. Until the assets exceed $250,000, there is no filing required at all. Yet a solo 401(k) has all the major tax advantages of a multiple-participant 401(k) plan: The before-tax contribution limits and tax treatment are identical."

SEP IRA

Officially known as a simplified employee pension, a SEP IRA is a variation on a traditional IRA.8 As the easiest plan to establish and operate, it's an excellent option for sole proprietors, though it also allows for one or more employees.

How it Works

The employer alone contributes to an SEP IRA—not employees. So, unlike the solo 401(k), you would only contribute wearing your employer hat. You can contribute up to 25% of your net earnings (defined as your annual profit less half of your self-employment taxes), up to a maximum of $58,000 in 2021.

The plan also offers flexibility to vary contributions, make them in a lump sum at the end of the year, or skip them altogether. There is no annual funding requirement.

Its simplicity and flexibility make the plan most desirable for one-person businesses, but there is a catch if you have people working for you. Although you do not have to contribute to the plan each year, when you do contribute, you need to do so for all your eligible employees—up to 25% of their compensation, limited to $290,000 annually.

While SEP IRAs are simple, they are not necessarily the most effective means of saving for retirement. "You can contribute more to a SEP IRA than a solo 401(k), excluding the profit-sharing, but you must make enough money since it's based on the percentage of profits," says Joseph Anderson, CFP, president of Pure Financial Advisors.

Setting it Up

The account is simpler to set up than a solo 401(k). You can easily open a SEP IRA online at brokerages such as TD Ameritrade or Fidelity Investments.

SIMPLE IRA

Officially known as the savings incentive match plan for employees, a SIMPLE IRA is kind of a cross between an IRA and a 401(k) plan. Although available to sole proprietors, it works best for small businesses. Companies with 100 or fewer employees that might find other sorts of plans too expensive.

How it Works

The SIMPLE IRA follows the same investment, rollover, and distribution rules as a traditional or SEP IRA, except for its lower contribution thresholds. You can put all your net earnings from self-employment in the plan, up to a maximum of $13,500 in 2021, plus an additional $3,000 if you are 50 or older.

Employees can contribute along with employers in the same annual amounts. As the employer, however, you are required to contribute dollar for dollar up to 3% of each participating employee's income to the plan each year or a fixed 2% contribution to every eligible employee's income whether they contribute or not.

Just like a 401(k) plan, the SIMPLE IRA is funded by taxdeductible employer contributions and pretax employee contributions. In a way, the employer's obligation is less. That is because employees make contributions even though there is that mandated matching. And the amount you (as the employer) can contribute for yourself is subject to the same contribution limit as the employees.

Early withdrawal penalties are particularly heavy at 25% within the first two years of the plan.

Setting it Up

As with other IRAs, you must open these plans with a financial institution, which have rules as to what kinds of investments can be purchased. They may also charge plan administration and participation fees. The process is like a SEP IRA, but the paperwork is more complicated.

Keogh Plan

The Keogh or HR 10 plan (more commonly referred to today as a qualified or profit-sharing plan) is arguably the most complex for self-employed workers. But it also allows for the most potential retirement savings.

How it Works

Keogh plans usually can take the form of a defined-contribution plan, in which a fixed sum or percentage is contributed every pay period. In 2021, these plans cap total contributions in a year at $58,000. Another option, though, allows them to be structured as defined-benefit plans. In 2021, the maximum annual benefit was set at $230,000 or 100% of the employee's compensation, whichever is lower.

A business must be unincorporated and set up as a sole proprietorship, limited liability company (LLC), or partnership to use a Keogh plan. Although all contributions are made on a pretax basis, there may be a vesting requirement. These plans benefit high earners, especially the defined-benefit version, which allows greater contributions than any other plan.

Setting it Up

Keogh Plans have federal filing requirements. This means complex paperwork, so you'll probably need professional help from an accountant, investment adviser, or a financial institution. Your options for custodians may be more limited than with other retirement plans, which means you will need a brick-and-mortar institution rather than an online-only service. Charles Schwab is one brokerage that offers and services these plans.

A Keogh is best suited for firms with a single high-earning boss or two and several lower-earning employees as in the case of a medical or legal practice.

Health Savings Account (HSA)

As a freelancer, you may have to pay for your own health insurance. The deductibles for individual medical plans tend to be high. If that's your situation, consider opening a health savings account (HSA). Though created for medical expenses rather than one's retirement years, an HSA can function as a de facto retirement account.

HSAs are funded with pretax dollars, and the money within them grows tax deferred as with an

IRA or a 401(k). While the funds are meant to be withdrawn for out-of-pocket medical costs, they do not have to be, so you can let them accumulate year after year. Once you reach age 65, you can withdraw them for any reason. If it is a medical one (either current or to reimburse yourself for old costs), it is still tax-free. If it's a non-medical expense, you are taxed at your current rate.

To open an HSA, you must be covered by a high-deductible health insurance plan (HDHP). For 2021, the IRS defines a high deductible as $1,400 per individual and $2,800 per family. Not all plans allow for HSAs. If yours does, in 2021 you are allowed to contribute up to $3,600 for an individual plan or $7,200 for a family plan. People over 50 are allowed a $1,000 catch-up contribution.

Traditional or Roth IRA

If none of the above plans seems a good fit, you can start your own individual IRA. Both Roth and traditional individual retirement accounts (IRAs) are available to anyone with employment income, and that includes freelancers. Roth IRAs let you contribute after-tax dollars, while traditional IRAs let you contribute pretax dollars. In 2021, the maximum annual contribution is $6,000, $7,000 if you are age 50 or older, or your total earned income, whichever is less.

Most freelancers work for someone else before striking out on their own. If you had a retirement plan such as a 401(k), 403(b), or 457(b) with a former employer, the best way to manage the accumulated savings is often to transfer them to a rollover IRA or, alternatively, a one-participant 401(k).

Rolling over allows you to choose how to invest the money, rather than being limited by the choices in an employer-sponsored plan. Also, the transferred sum can jump-start you into saving in your new entrepreneurial career.

Managing Your Retirement Funds

Make no mistake, you need to start saving for retirement as soon as you start earning income, even if you cannot afford much at the beginning. The sooner you start, the more you will accumulate, thanks to the miracle of compounding.

Let's say you save $40 per month and invest that money at a 3.69% rate of return, which is what the Vanguard Total Bond Market Index Fund earned across a 10-year period ending in December 2020.15 Using an online savings calculator, an initial amount of $40 plus $40 per month for 30 years adds up to just under $26,500. Raise the rate to 13.66%, the average yield of the Vanguard Total Stock Market Index Fund over the same period, and the number rises to more than $207,000.1

As your savings build, you may want to get the help of a financial advisor to determine the best way to apportion your funds. Some companies even offer free or low-cost retirement planning advice to clients. Robo-advisors such as Betterment and Wealthfront provide automated planning and portfolio building as a low-cost alternative to human financial advisors.

The Bottom Line

Creating a retirement strategy is vitally important when you are a freelancer because there is no one looking out for your retirement but you. That is why your mantra should be pay yourself first.

Many people think of retirement money as the money they put away if there is any cash left at the end of the month or year. "That's paying yourself last," says David Blaylock, CFP, director of financial planning at Kindur. "Paying yourself first means saving before you do anything else. Try and set aside a certain portion of your income the day you get paid before you spend any discretionary money."

How Social Security Works for the Self-Employed

You still must pay into the system

When you work for someone else, that employer takes Social Security taxes out of your paycheck and sends the money to the Internal Revenue Service (IRS).1 But things work a little differently for people who are self-employed. If you fall into this category, keep reading. This article will help you understand how to calculate the Social Security taxes you owe.

Key Takeaways

- Self-employed workers must pay both the employee and employer portions of Social Security taxes.

- Reducing your income by taking every available deduction will reduce your taxes, but it will also reduce the size of your Social Security benefit payment in retirement.

- The amount of your Social Security benefit payment is calculated based on your 35 highest-earning years.

Understanding Social Security Taxes

If you work for someone else, Social Security taxes are deducted from your paycheck. The Social Security tax rate for 2021 is 6.2%, plus 1.45% for the Medicare tax.2 So, if your annual salary is $50,000, the amount that will go to Social Security over the course of the year is $3,100, plus $725, for a total of $3,825.

Your employer will match an additional $3,825 over the course of the year, and it will also report your Social Security wages to the government. When you retire or if you become disabled, the government uses your history of Social Security wages and tax credits to calculate the benefit payments you'll receive.

What Happens When You're Self-Employed?

When you are self-employed, you are considered both the employee and the employer. This means it is your responsibility to withhold Social Security from your earnings, contributing the employer's matching portion of Social Security and the individual's portion. Instead of withholding Social Security taxes from each paycheck—many self-employed people don't get regular paychecks, after all—you pay all the Social Security taxes on your earnings when you file your annual federal income tax return. This amounts to both your personal contribution and your business's contribution.

IRS Schedule SE: Self-Employment Tax is where you report your business's net profit or loss as calculated on Schedule C. The federal government uses this information to calculate the Social Security benefits you will be entitled to later down the road. Self-employment tax consists of both the employee and employer portion of Social Security (6.2% + 6.2% = 12.4%) and the employee and employer portion of Medicare (1.45% + 1.45% = 2.9%), which makes the total self-employment tax rate 15.3%.

It may seem like you are getting the short end of the stick because you must pay both the employee and the employer portion of the tax, but that is not necessarily true.

If you are self-employed and earned $400 or less, you will not owe Social Security taxes.

Self-Employed Tax Deductions

If you are self-employed, how much you pay in Social Security taxes is based on your net income. On Schedule SE, you multiply your business' net profit or loss as calculated on Schedule C by 92.35% before calculating how much self-employment tax you owe.4

If your Schedule C profit was $100,000, you would only pay the 12.4% combined employee and employer portion of Social Security tax on $92,350. Instead of paying $12,400, you would pay $11,451.40. This tax deduction would save you $948.60. Half of $11,451.40 is $5,725.70, which represents the employer's matching portion of the Social Security tax. It is considered a business expense and reduces your tax liability.

You report it on line 14 of Schedule 1: Additional Income and Adjustments to Income, and you subtract it from line 6 of page 2 of Form 1040, marked total income. This business expense would reduce your taxable earnings to $94,274.30, which you enter on line 7 or adjusted gross income.

Your total amount of self-employment tax, $11,451.40, is reported on line 4 of Schedule 2: Additional Taxes. You then report any other taxes—there are eight categories—on the same form, total them all, and list that total on line 10. In our example, there are no other taxes, so that amount is still $11,451.40.8 This is then entered on line 15 of page 2 of Form 1040, marked "Other taxes, including self-employment tax, from Schedule 2, line 10." Of course, you also must pay regular income tax on your profit.

The CARES (Coronavirus Aid, Relief, and Economic Security) Act allows employers to defer employee Social Security taxes through Dec. 31, 2020—50% of the deferred amount will be due Dec. 31, 2021, and the other half by Dec. 31, 2022. This applies to the self-employed, too.

How Minimizing Taxes Minimizes Benefits

There are many business expenses that can reduce your tax liability besides the Social Security tax deductions you can take when you're self-employed.

"Business expenses reduce your overall tax, which ultimately lowers your Social Security taxes. Business tax deductions are a way of minimizing self-employment tax and Social Security taxes," says Carlos Dias Jr., founder and managing partner of Dias Wealth LLC in Lake Mary, Fla.

But keep in mind that this can work against you when it comes to Social Security benefit calculations, which are based in part on your taxable earnings. Here is why. The more deductions you have, the lower your Schedule C income. Lowering your Schedule C income is an effective way to reduce how much federal, state, and local income tax you owe. However, this lower amount becomes part of your Social Security earnings history and means you may receive lower benefits in retirement than if you didn't take those deductions.

Minimize Taxes Now or Maximize Benefits Later?

Should you skip some or all the business tax deductions you are entitled to in order to increase your future Social Security benefit? Maybe. The answer is complicated because lower-earning business people stand to gain more in the future than their higher-earning counterparts due to the way Social Security retirement benefits are calculated.

Another crucial factor is where your Schedule C earnings fall compared to your previous years' earnings. If you have a full 35-year career behind you and you are not earning as much in your current self-employed pursuits, it makes sense to take all the deductions you can, as your Social Security benefits will be calculated based on your 35 highest-earning years. In this case, you want to minimize your Social Security taxes.

But if you are currently in the high-earning part of your career, a higher Schedule C income can help you get higher Social Security benefits later. Unless you enjoy complex math, problems or have a top-notch accountant, it is not worth the headache to figure out whether you will earn more in future Social Security benefits than you would save by claiming all the deductions you can today.

Of course, if you're on the cusp of not having enough Schedule C income to give you the work credits you need to qualify for Social Security, it may be worth foregoing some deductions to make sure you're entitled to any benefits at all.

How Much Control Do You Want?

As we don't know what Social Security benefit payments will look like in the future—many people expect them to be lower because of how the system is funded—you may want to go with the sure thing and take the lower tax liability today. After all, one way to lower your tax liability is to take money out of your business and put it in one of the available retirement plans for the self-employed. That is money you will have a lot more control over than Social Security benefits.

"The great thing about Social Security is you cannot access it until retirement age," says Kevin Michels, CFP, EA, financial planner and president of Medicus Wealth Planning.

"You can't make early withdrawals, [but] you can't skip payments, and you are guaranteed a benefit," Michels adds. "However, you have only a small say in the future legislation of Social Security and how it will be affected by the mismanagement of government funds."

Michels continues to say the following:

If you have trouble saving for retirement already, then paying [as much as allowed] into Social Security may be the better option. If you are confident you can stick to a savings plan, invest wisely, and not touch your savings until retirement, it may be a better idea to minimize what you pay into Social Security and take more responsibility for your retirement.

If You Fail to File

If you don't file a tax return reporting your self-employment income, you have a limited time to file a return and still get credit with the Social Security Administration (SSA) for your work time and income. You must file the return within three years, three months, and 15 days after the tax year for which you earned the income for which you want credit.

That means if you did not file a return reporting your 2019 self-employment income, you would have until April 15, 2023, to correct it. However, this grace period does not exempt you from any penalties and back taxes you may owe because of filing late.

When You Don't Have to Pay Social Security Taxes

You do not owe Social Security taxes on the portion of your wages that exceed a certain earnings threshold. The wage base for 2021 is $142,800 (up from $137,700 in 2020), and you don't owe Social Security taxes on the portion of your earnings that exceed that amount.

Let us say your annual earnings were $145,000. The percentage of taxes you owe would be applied up to the first $142,800 but not on the $2,200 above that. This annual cap on Social Security taxes also applies to employees who work for someone else.

6%

The percentage of American taxpayers who exceeded the tax cap since 1983.

Qualifying for Social Security Benefits

Anyone born in 1929 or later needs 40 Social Security work credits, the equivalent of 10 years of work, to qualify for Social Security benefits. For every quarter that you earn at least $1,470 in 2021 (which was $1,410 in 2020), you earn one credit. The number changes annually.

Even if your business is not particularly successful, or you only work part-time or occasionally, it is not difficult to earn the Social Security credits you need. In fact, even if your earnings fall below this threshold or if your business has a loss, there are some alternative ways to earn Social Security credits. These optional methods may increase the amount of self-employment tax you owe, but they will help you get the work credits you need.

Your eventual benefit payments do take your earnings into account. If you never earned much money from a lifetime of self-employment, do not count on getting a large Social Security check in retirement. If you started claiming benefits this year, for example, and your average monthly earnings worked out to just $800, your monthly Social Security retirement benefit would be $720—assuming you're at full retirement age. That is not much, but if you managed to get by on an average of $800 a month during your working years, you could work with a monthly benefit payment of $720 in retirement.

Certain categories of earnings don't count toward Social Security for most people, such as stock dividends, loan interest, and real estate income. This means you do not pay Social Security taxes on this income, and it also is not used to calculate your future benefits. The exception is if your business operates in one of these areas that do not count—self-employed stockbrokers, for example, do count stock dividends toward their Social Security earnings.

The Bottom Line

Social Security really is not much different whether you are self-employed or work for someone else. Self-employed individuals earn Social Security work credits the same way employees do and qualify for benefits based on their work credits and earnings.

Business tax deductions create the biggest difference. If you work for someone else, you pay Social Security taxes on all your earnings, up to the $142,800 cap in 2021. But if you work for yourself, deductions you claim on Schedule C can make your taxable income lower. That can decrease your Social Security taxes today, but also potentially decreases your Social Security benefits later.

Saving for Retirement When You Don't Have a Regular Job

You don't need to be employed to save for retirement

Many people find themselves outside of the formal workforce from time to time. Some end up unemployed by choice while others find themselves without work because of layoffs. These individuals have several options available to them to keep the income flowing. For instance, some may join the gig economy while others try consulting, freelancing, or staying home to care for their family.

When people stop picking up a regular paycheck, they often stop contributing to their retirement savings. This is not wise. Keeping up those contributions, however small, can make a significant difference in the income you have after retirement. This article looks at some of the ways to keep that retirement account growing even when you do not have a steady source of income.

Key Takeaways

- Self-employed people can invest in a solo 401(k), which has higher contribution limits than the 401(k) version that employers offer.

- A non-employed spouse can contribute to an IRA if their spouse has taxable income.

- Health savings accounts are designed to pay for medical expenses, but after you reach 65, that restriction no longer applies.

Saving for Retirement Without a Paycheck

Although it's true that the majority of working people save for retirement via an employer-sponsored program, you can do it on your own.1 It's easier than you think to save money without a regular paycheck. And you do not need regular employment to get the tax advantages that come with many plans.

There are a number of ways to use existing retirement-savings vehicles to save independent of an employer, including a solo 401(k), spousal individual retirement account (IRA), and health savings account (HSA).

Solo 401(k)

The solo 401(k), also known as the independent 401(k), is designed for people who are self-employed as sole proprietors, independent contractors, or members of a partnership. It is for people who work on their own or with a spouse, and who do not have employees. The contributions combine deferred income and profit-sharing elements.

In 2021, you may contribute up to $19,500 to a solo 401(k). Individuals age 50 and older can contribute an additional catch-up contribution of $6,500.

Allowable Contributions for a Solo 401(k)

The profit-sharing component for a sole proprietor is 20% of self-employment income reduced by 50% of self-employment taxes. For incorporated businesses, the profit-sharing component increases to 25% of self-employment income with no deduction for self-employment taxes.4

In 2021, that brings the total amount of allowable contributions in deferrals and profit-sharing to $58,000 a year, or $64,500 including catch-up contributions.

Example of a Solo 401(k)

Let us say that Mary, a 33-year-old marketing manager, left her full-time job when she had a baby. She does some consulting work and earns $20,000 in a year. As the owner of a sole proprietorship, she could put away up to $19,500 from her earnings in employee deferrals in 2021.

Solo 401(k) plans must be established before December 31 of the tax year for contributions to be allowed for the upcoming year.

Spousal IRA

A nonworking spouse who files jointly has the option of investing in either a traditional or a Roth spousal IRA as long as their spouse has taxable compensation. The maximum contribution for 2020 and 2021 for either IRA is $6,000, plus an additional $1,000 for individuals age 50 and older. This allows the family to double its IRA retirement savings.

Allowable Contributions for a Spousal IRA: Tax-Filing Status Matters

Keep in mind that your filing status can affect the level of allowable contributions. Let us say Joe, 51, lost his job late in 2019 and has not been able to find full-time work during 2020, but wants to continue to contribute toward his retirement. His spouse has taxable compensation of $50,000 for 2020.

If Joe and his wife filed separately, he would be unable to contribute any amount to an IRA for 2020 because he had no taxable compensation that year. If they filed separately and he had taxable earnings of only $2,000 for 2020, his IRA contribution would be limited to $2,000.

Example of a Spousal IRA

Here is what happens if Joe and his wife file jointly. With the wife's $50,000 income, Joe could contribute a total of $7,000 to an IRA for 2020 and has until April 15, 2021, to do so. That is the standard $6,000 contribution plus a $1,000 catch-up contribution for those aged 50 or older. You can contribute to an IRA as late as April 15 of the following year.

Health Savings Account (HSA)

A health savings account (HSA) is another option. An HSA is a tax-advantaged account that allows you to pay non-covered medical expenses. HSAs are available to individuals with a high-deductible health plan (HDHP).

For people who are employed, both the employer and the employee may contribute to the account. Those who are not employed may contribute on their own behalf. And those contributions are eligible for a tax deduction.

Allowable Contributions for an HSA

The maximum contribution to an HSA for 2021 is $3,600 for an individual and $7,200 for a family. Additional catch-up contributions of $1,000 are allowed for people 55 years of age or older.

Can You Use an HSA for Retirement Savings?

Yes, you can. Distributions used for qualified medical expenses are tax-free at any age. Distributions that are not used for medical expenses are counted as income and are taxable. In addition, depending on your age, they can be subject to a 20% penalty.

But if you keep these funds in the HSA and begin withdrawing them at the age of 65 or older, you can use it for any purpose, just like a traditional IRA. Like a traditional IRA, you will owe income tax on the money, but no penalties. Penalty-free IRA withdrawals begin at age 59½.

The money deposited to an HSA does not have to come from earned income. It can come from savings, stock dividends, unemployment compensation, or even welfare payments.

Saving for Retirement via a Brokerage Account

You can always invest for your retirement through a brokerage account. The earnings will not be tax-deferred, but you will be increasing the pot of money that can provide you with a source of income during your retirement.

This can be an excellent way to invest money once you exhaust your tax-deferred contribution amounts. In addition, since withdrawals from a taxable account are not taxable again (you have already paid), an investment account gives you added tax-planning flexibility that can be helpful.

The Bottom Line

Saving for retirement without a regular paycheck is possible. You have several options to choose from that offer tax advantages.

For those who are eligible, solo 401(k)s, spousal IRAs, and HSAs can help build a retirement nest egg. Investments in a brokerage account, while not tax-deferred, can help grow retirement savings, too. Regardless of which route you choose, start saving for retirement as early as possible so your money has more time to grow.

Simplified Employee Pension (SEP)

What Is a Simplified Employee Pension (SEP)?

A simplified employee pension (SEP) is an individual retirement account (IRA) that an employer or a self-employed person can establish. The employer is allowed a tax deduction for contributions made to a SEP IRA and makes contributions to each eligible employee's plan on a discretionary basis.

Additionally, under the Setting Every Community Up for Retirement Enhancement (SECURE) Act, which was enacted on Dec. 20, 2019, small employers get a tax credit to offset the costs of starting a 401(k) plan or SIMPLE IRA with auto-enrollment. That is on top of the start-up credit they already receive.

SEP IRAs often have higher annual contribution limits than standard IRAs. Fundamentally, a SEP IRA can be considered a traditional IRA with the ability to receive employer contributions. One major benefit it offers employees is that employer contributions are vested immediately.

Key Takeaways

- A simplified employee pension (SEP) is an individual retirement account (IRA) that an employer or self-employed individual can establish.

- SEP IRAs are used by small businesses and self-employed individuals to meet their retirement savings needs.

- SEP IRA contribution limits are annual and often higher than standard IRAs and 401(k)s.

SEP Account: Jessica Perez

How a Simplified Employee Pension (SEP) Works

A SEP IRA is an attractive option for many business owners because it does not come with many of the start-up and operating costs of most conventional employer-sponsored retirement plans. Many employers also set up a SEP IRA to contribute to their own retirement at higher levels than a traditional IRA allows.

Small organizations favor SEP IRAs because of eligibility requirements for contributors, including a minimum age of 21, at least three years of employment, and a $600 compensation minimum. In addition, a SEP IRA allows employers to skip contributions during years when business is down.

SEP IRAs are treated like traditional IRAs for tax purposes and allow the same investment options. The same transfer and rollover rules that apply to traditional IRAs also apply to SEP IRAs.9 When an employer makes contributions to SEP IRA accounts, it receives a tax deduction for the amount contributed. Additionally, the business is not locked into an annual contribution—decisions about whether to contribute and how much can change each year.

The employer is not responsible for making investment decisions. Instead, the IRA trustee determines eligible investments, and the individual employee account owners make specific investment decisions. The trustee also deposits contributions, sends annual statements, and files all required documents with the IRS.

Immediate vesting

Contributions to SEP IRAs are immediately 100% vested, and the IRA owner directs the investments.7 An eligible employee (including the business owner) who participates in their employer's SEP plan must establish a traditional IRA to which the employer will deposit SEP contributions.

Some financial institutions require the traditional IRA to be labeled as a SEP IRA before they will allow the account to receive SEP contributions. Others will allow SEP contributions to be deposited to a traditional IRA regardless of whether the IRA is labeled as a SEP IRA.

Contributions to a SEP IRA are immediately 100% vested, and account owners must choose their investments themselves from a list provided by the account trustee.

SEP IRA Contribution Limits

Contributions made by employers cannot exceed the lesser of 25% of an employee's compensation or $58,000 in 2021 (up from $57,000 in 2020).12 13 As with a traditional IRA, withdrawals from SEP IRAs in retirement are taxed as ordinary income.

When a business is a sole proprietorship, the employee-owner pays themselves wages and may also make a SEP contribution, which is limited to 25% of wages (or profits) minus the SEP contribution. For a particular contribution rate (CR), the reduced rate is CR ÷ (1 + CR) for a 25% contribution rate. This yields a 20% reduced rate, as in the above example.

Because the funding vehicle for a SEP plan is a traditional IRA, SEP contributions, once deposited, become traditional IRA assets and are subject to many of the traditional IRA rules, including the following:

- Distribution rules

- Investment rules

- Contribution and deduction rules for traditional IRA contributions, which apply to the employee's regular IRA contributions, not the SEP employer contributions

- Documentation requirements for establishing an IRA

In addition to the documents required for establishing a SEP plan (discussed later), each SEP IRA must meet the documentation requirements for a traditional IRA.

$290,000

The compensation limit for a business to be allowed to set up a SEP IRA in 2021 ($285,000 for 2020).

SEP IRA Rules

Not all businesses can start SEP IRAs, which were primarily designed to encourage retirement benefits among businesses that would otherwise not set up employer-sponsored plans. Sole proprietors, partnerships, and corporations can establish SEPs. Too high an income can be a limitation—the 2020 eligible compensation limit is $285,000 (up from $280,000 in 2019 and rising to $290,000 in 2021).2 13 Unlike qualified retirement plans—under which participants, including the business owner, may borrow up to the lesser of 50% or $50,000 of their vested balance—the SEP does not have this feature.

Moreover, certain types of employees may be excluded by their employer from participating in a SEP IRA, even if they would otherwise be eligible based on the plan's rules. Workers who are covered in a union collective bargaining agreement for retirement benefits, for example, can be excluded. Workers who are nonresident aliens can also be excluded if they do not receive U.S. wages or other service compensation from the employer.

SEP contributions and earnings are held in SEP IRAs and can be withdrawn at any time, subject to the general limitations imposed on traditional IRAs. A withdrawal is taxable in the year received. If a participant makes a withdrawal before age 59½, a 10% additional tax applies.

SEP contributions and earnings may be rolled over tax free to other IRAs and retirement plans. SEP contributions and earnings must eventually be distributed following the IRA-required minimum distributions rules.

SEP IRA vs. Individual 401(k)

A SEP IRA and an individual 401(k), also known as a solo 401(k), are both retirement accounts that allow employer contributions. They have two main differences.

The first is that although the maximum contribution limit for both is comparable once income levels reach $200,000, you can contribute more to a 401(k) at lower income levels than you can to a SEP IRA. In addition, if you are 50 or older, the 401(k) has a catch-up contribution, which the SEP IRA does not. The second significant difference is that you can take a loan against the 401(k), something that is not allowed with a SEP IRA.

A SEP IRA, however, is easier to set up and maintain. An individual 401(k) requires its owner to be more involved in its administrative responsibilities, and it can also generate higher fees than a SEP IRA.

SEP IRA vs. Traditional IRA vs. Roth IRA

There are important differences among these three retirement accounts. With a traditional IRA, you contribute tax-free money, which reduces your tax bill in the year in which you make the contribution. However, when you withdraw funds in retirement, they are taxed as ordinary income, and you are required to make distributions once you reach the age of 72.20 This makes it best for people who expect to be in a lower tax bracket when they retire.

A Roth IRA reverses the process. You have already paid income tax on the money you contribute, so withdrawals in retirement are tax free. This makes a Roth IRA better for people who expect to be in a higher tax bracket in retirement. In addition, there are no required minimum distributions from a Roth IRA, so if you do not need the money, you can just let it sit there and pass the account on to your heirs.

A SEP IRA is, of course, only available to self-employed persons. It allows employer contributions, which traditional and Roth IRAs do not, and all contributions to it are tax free, meaning that distributions in retirement will be taxed as ordinary income. The maximum contribution limit for a SEP IRA is considerable higher than that for either a traditional or Roth IRA. Employers can get a tax deduction for their contribution, which means when the self-employed person is both employer and employee, they can get that tax deduction. SEP IRAs were invented to help small businesses provide employer-sponsored retirement plans to their employees and owners.

A 401(k) Plan for the Small Business Owner

The solo 401(k) plan is worth a look

What Is a Solo 401(k)?

The 401(k) plan has gained popularity among small business owners ever since 2001, when some changes to federal tax law made it a better and more flexible choice for their needs compared with some other retirement savings options. These 401(k) plans are known as solo 401(k) or self-employed 401(k) plans.

It is a retirement savings option for small businesses whose only eligible participants in the plan are the business owners (and their spouses, if they are also employed by the business). It can be a smart way for someone who is a sole proprietor or an independent contractor to set aside a decent-sized nest egg for retirement.

Key Takeaways

- A solo 401(k) plan—also called a self-employed 401(k)—is for businesses whose only eligible participants in the plan are its owners (and spouses).

- These plans are often less complicated and cost less to set up.

- If you have non-owner employees, they must not meet the eligibility requirements you select for the plan.

- There are two components to a solo 401(k) plan: employee elective-deferral contributions and profit-sharing contributions.

- A solo 401(k)s may also offer loans, does not require nondiscrimination testing, and allows for the deduction of plan contributions of up to 25% of eligible compensation.

A 401(k) by Any Other Name

Not content with the federal acronym, various financial institutions have their own names for the solo 401(k) plan. The independent 401(k) is one of the most generic. Other examples include:

- The Individual(k)

- Solo 401(k) or Solo-k

- Uni-k Plan

- One-Participant k

- Self-Employed 401(k)1

If you are not sure which name your financial service provider uses, ask about the 401(k) plan for small business owners. The Internal Revenue Service (IRS) provides a handy primer on such plans.1

Who Is Eligible for Individual 401(k) Plans?

A common misconception about the solo 401(k) is that it can be used only by sole proprietors. In fact, the solo 401(k) plan may be used by any small businesses, including corporations, limited liability companies (LLCs), and partnerships. The only limitation is that the only eligible plan participants are the business owners and their spouses, provided they are employed by the business.

A person who works for one company (in which they have no ownership) and participates in its 401(k) can also establish a solo 401(k) for a small business they run on the side, funding it with earnings from that venture. However, the aggregate annual contributions to both plans cannot collectively exceed the IRS-established maximums.

Simpler Documentation Requirements

For small business owners who meet certain requirements, most financial institutions that offer retirement plan products have developed truncated versions of the regular 401(k) plan for use by business owners who want to adopt the solo 401(k). As a result, less-complex documentation is needed to establish the plan. Fees may also be low. Make sure to receive the proper documentation from your financial services provider.

Choose Your Eligibility Requirements

As noted above, the solo 401(k) plan may be adopted only by businesses in which the only employees eligible to participate in the plan are the business owners and eligible spouses. For eligibility purposes, a spouse is considered an owner of the business, so if a spouse is employed by the business, you are still eligible to adopt the solo 401(k).

If your business has non-owner employees who are eligible to participate in the plan, your business may not adopt the solo 401(k) plan. Therefore, if you have non-owner employees, they must not meet the eligibility requirements you select for the plan, which must remain within the following limitations.

Nonresident Aliens

You may exclude nonresident aliens who receive no U.S. income and those who receive benefits under a collective-bargaining agreement.

Years of Service

- **For 401(k) Employee Elective-Deferral Contributions:** You may require an employee to perform one year of service before becoming eligible to make elective-deferral contributions.

- **For Profit-Sharing Contributions:** You may require an employee to perform up to two years of service in order to be eligible to receive profit-sharing contributions. However, most solo 401(k) plans will limit this requirement to one year.

- **For Plan Purposes:** An employee is considered to have performed one year of service if they work at least 1,000 hours during the year. While you may choose to require fewer than 1,000 hours under a regular qualified plan, most solo 401(k) plans include a hard-coded limit of 1,000 hours.

The Wrong Requirements

Setting the wrong eligibility requirements could result in you being excluded from the plan or non-owner employees being eligible to participate in the plan.

For example, say you elect zero years of service as a requirement to participate, but you have five seasonal employees who work fewer than 1,000 hours each year. These employees would be eligible to participate in the plan because they meet the age and service requirements. Consequently, their eligibility would disqualify your business from being suitable to adopt the solo 401(k) plan. Instead, you could adopt a regular 401(k) plan.

Some solo 401(k) products, by definition, require further exclusions. Before you decide to establish a solo 401(k) plan, be sure to check with your financial services provider regarding its provisions.

Solo 401(k) Plan Components

There are two components to the solo 401(k) plan: employee elective-deferral contributions and profit-sharing contributions.

- **Employee Contribution Limits:** You may make a salary-deferral contribution of up to 100% of your compensation but no more than the annual limit for the year. For both 2020 and 2021, the limit is $19,500, plus $6,500 for people age 50 or over.

- **Employer Contribution Limits:** The business may contribute up to 25% of your compensation (20% in the case of a sole proprietor or a Schedule C taxpayer) but no more than $58,000 for 2021 ($57,000 for 2021). An employee age 50 or above can still contribute an additional $6,500 for 2020 and 2021.3

Solo Contributions vs. Other Plans

In comparison with other popular retirement plans, the solo 401(k) plan has high contribution limits as outlined above, which is the key component that attracts owners of small businesses. Some other retirement plans also limit the contributions by employers or set lower limits on salary-deferred contributions.

The following is a summary of contribution comparisons for the employer plans used by small businesses.

Account	Elective Deferral	Maximum Employer Contribution	Catch-Up Contribution
Solo 401(k)	$19,500 for 2020 and 2021	25% of compensation or 20% in the case of a sole proprietor or a Schedule C taxpayer	$6,500 for 2020 and 2021
SEP IRA	Not Allowed	25% of compensation or 20% of modified net profit for unincorporated business owners	Not Allowed
Profit-Sharing or Money-Purchase Pension Plan	Not Allowed	25% of compensation or 20% of modified net profit for unincorporated business owners	Not Allowed
SIMPLE IRA	$13,500 for 2020 and 2021	3% of compensation/income	$3,000 for 2020 and 2021

The Calculation

As mentioned earlier, you may make employee elective-deferral contributions of up to 100% of your compensation but no more than the elective-deferral limit for the year. Profit-sharing contributions are limited to 25% of your compensation (or 20% of your modified net profit if your business is a sole proprietorship or partnership).4

The total solo 401(k) contribution is the employee elective-deferral contribution plus the profit-sharing contribution of up to $57,000 for 2020 and $58,000 for 2021.

If your business is a corporation, the profit-sharing contribution is based on W-2 wages you receive. If you receive $70,000 in W-2 wages, for instance, your profit-sharing contribution could be up to $17,500 ($70,000 x 25%). When added to a salary-deferral contribution of $19,000, the total would be $36,500.

If your business is a sole proprietorship or partnership, the calculation gets a little more involved. In this case your profit-sharing contribution is based on your modified net profit and is limited to

20%. The IRS provides a step-by-step formula for determining your modified net profit in IRS Publication 560.

In response to the COVID-19 pandemic, the IRS extended numerous 2020 deadlines for filing and paying taxes, though those extensions have been surpassed.6 Still, as of the end of October 2020, the IRS continues to update COVID-19 relief, so check the website for the latest developments.

Other Benefits of the Solo 401(k)

There are a number of other benefits that come with the Solo 401(k).

Loans

As with other qualified plans, you may be able to borrow from the solo 401(k) up to (1) the greater of $10,000 or 50% of the balance or (2) $50,000, whichever is less. Check the plan document to determine if any other limitations apply.

5500 Filing May Not Be Required

Because the plan covers only the business owner, you may not be required to file Form 5500 series return unless your balance exceeds $250,000.

No Nondiscrimination Testing

Certain nondiscrimination testing must be performed for 401(k) plans. These tests ensure that the business owners and higher-paid employees do not receive an inequitably high amount of contribution when compared with lower-paid employees.

Such tests can be overly complex and may require the services of an experienced plan administrator, which can be costly. Because the solo 401(k) plan covers only the business owner, there is no one against whom you can discriminate, so these tests are not required.

Deducting Contributions

Like other employer plans, the solo 401(k) allows you to deduct plan contributions of up to 25% of eligible compensation. For plan purposes, compensation is limited to $285,000 in 2020 and $290,000 in 2021. Earnings of more than that amount are disregarded for plan purposes.

Other Considerations

If you own more than one business, you must check with your tax professional to determine whether you are eligible to adopt the solo 401(k). Ownership in another business that covers employees other than the business owner could result in your being ineligible for this type of plan.

Solo 401(k) vs. SEP: Which Is Best for Business

Owners?

Look at the differences between these retirement savings plans

Small business owners have several options to choose from when it comes to retirement planning. Traditional or Roth IRAs can provide a good start on saving for retirement, but successful business owners often need a plan that allows them to defer much larger amounts on an annual basis.

SEP IRAs were introduced as a way to let small business owners establish a retirement account for their businesses without the headaches that come with ERISA-sponsored plans.1 However, subsequent financial legislation created the solo 401(k), which also offers a simplified way for business owners to save for retirement and enjoy some of the benefits of a 401(k) plan that are not available with SEPs. Here's a look at these two types of plans and how they serve the needs of small businesses.

Key Takeaways

- SEP IRAs and solo 401(k)s both allow small business owners to establish retirement accounts for their employees.

- SEP IRAs are funded by employer contributions alone.

- Solo 401(k)s allow both employer and employee contributions.

How Self-Employed Retirement Plans Work

SEP IRAs have been around for decades, and they are probably still the simplest way for business owners to save for retirement. These plans are purely profit-sharing in nature and allow owners to make contributions for themselves and all eligible employees.

The amount that can be contributed is the lesser of up to 25% of business revenue—20% in the case of a sole proprietorship or a single-member limited liability corporation (LLC)—or $57,000 for 2020 and $58,000 for 2021. One of the main advantages of SEPs is their relative simplicity compared with the rigorous reporting requirements that come with qualified plans, even those that are designed for self-employed persons, such as Keogh plans.

Solo 401(k) plans are a relatively recent addition to the retirement plan community. These plans are designed exclusively for sole proprietorships that have only one employee (the owner). Also known as an "individual" or "self-employed" 401(k) plan, this type of retirement savings account is considered a better option for solo practitioners than a SEP IRA because it also offers the following features:

- **Employee deferrals** – Unlike SEP plans, solo 401(k)s allow participants to make a separate employee contribution as well as a profit-sharing contribution. This allows the proprietor to contribute up to $19,500 into the plan for 2020 and for 2021, even if the business loses money in those years.

- **Catch-up contributions** – A solo 401(k) allows the same amount to be contributed by the owner as a SEP (see limits above), but it also allows participants who are age 50 and above to contribute an additional $6,500 for 2020 and for 2021 as catch-up contributions.

- **Roth contributions** – Solo 401(k) plans allow for post-tax Roth contributions, which can allow the owner to accumulate a substantial pool of tax-free money over time. SEP IRAs only allow traditional pretax contributions.

- **Loan provision** – Solo 401(k) plans can allow participants to take out a loan equal to the lesser of 50% of the plan balance or $50,000. Loans are not available with SEP plans.

However, SEP IRAs do allow employers to make retirement plan contributions on behalf of employees, though they are allowed to exclude part-time workers, those under age 21, and those who have not worked for the employer in at least two of the previous five years.

Contribution limits are the same as for the owner, except that it is the lesser of the dollar limit or 25% of the employee's total compensation. SEP IRAs can also be established at any time before the business owner files a tax return, while solo 401(k) contributions must be made by Dec. 31 of the previous year in order to be counted on the return.

Solo 401(k) vs. SEP IRA: Key Differences							
	Employer	Employee	Catch-Up	Roth	Loan		Operational
SEP IRA	Yes	No	No	No	No	Anytime before filing tax return	Relatively simple
Solo 401(k)	Yes	Yes	Yes	Yes	Yes	Dec. 31 of the tax year	Rigorous reporting

(As of Oct. 30, 2020)

Which Should I Choose? SEP IRA vs. Solo 401(k)

Owners of small businesses have more choices today when it comes to saving for retirement. Those who have full-time employees can save for retirement using a SEP IRA, while solo practitioners can choose between that and a solo 401(k) plan that has higher contribution limits and other advantages.

For more information on retirement plans and accounts, download Publications 575, 590-A, and 590-B from the IRS website or consult your financial advisor.

CPSIA information can be obtained
at www.ICGtesting.com
Printed in the USA
LVHW060620200822
726395LV00014B/287